CW00499911

The Nation That Forgot God

The Nation That Forgot God

A BOOK OF ESSAYS

Edited by Edward Leigh and Alex Haydon

THE SOCIAL AFFAIRS UNIT

© The Social Affairs Unit 2009
All rights reserved

British Library Cataloguing in Publication Data
A catalogue record of this book is available from the British Library

All views expressed in this publication are those of the author, not those of the Social Affairs Unit, its Trustees, Advisers or Director

Printed and bound in the United Kingdom

ISBN-13: 978-1-904863-41-0

Social Affairs Unit
314–322 Regent Street
London W1B 5SA
www.socialaffairsunit.org.uk

The Social Affairs Unit has no responsibility for the persistence or accuracy of URLs for websites referred to in this publication, and does not guarantee that any content on such websites is, or will remain, accurate or appropriate.

CONTENTS

Introduction	The virtues of 'Assumism' *Edward Leigh*	7
CHAPTER 1	Grave symptoms *Edward Leigh*	11
CHAPTER 2	PC also stands for post-Christian *Alexander Boot*	22
CHAPTER 3	Make your own hope *Peter Mullen*	37
CHAPTER 4	Thinking and acting morally *Bishop Michael Nazir-Ali*	53
CHAPTER 5	Quo vadis? *Roger Scruton*	68
CHAPTER 6	The ambiguities of multiculturalism *Bat Ye'or*	82
CHAPTER 7	'Taught by no professors and illustrated by no examples': the British abolition of slavery *Canon Peter Williams*	99
CHAPTER 8	Christians and Muslims in Britain *Shusha Guppy*	115
CHAPTER 9	Shoring up the foundations: supporting traditional marriage and the family? *Philippa Taylor*	131

CHAPTER 10	To teach or not to teach *John Marks*	155
CHAPTER 11	Community cohesion and Catholic education *Archbishop Vincent Nichols*	177
CHAPTER 12	Seeking God: reflections on a hidden tradition *Abbot Aidan Bellenger*	189

Contributors biographies 196

Notes 203

INTRODUCTION

THE VIRTUES OF 'ASSUMISM'

EDWARD LEIGH

> Righteousness exalteth a nation.
>
> The Book of Proverbs

> The function of Christianity is not to reform or devise economic or social systems: her function is to reform and transform the economists themselves. The Church... is well aware that a change in social conditions, unaccompanied by a change in the dispositions of men, will but result in the substitution of one set of wrongdoers for another.
>
> Rev. Edward Leen, *Why the Cross?*, 1941

> And all that is ill you may repair if you walk together in humble repentance, expiating the sins of your fathers;
> And all that was good you must fight to keep with hearts as devoted as those of your fathers who fought to gain it.
>
> T. S. Eliot, *Choruses from 'The Rock'*, 1934, in *The Complete Poems and Plays of T.S. Eliot*, 1969

> Qui ne geule pas la verite, quand il sait la verite, se fait le complice des menteurs et des faussaires.
> ('He who does not bellow the truth when he knows the truth makes himself the accomplice of liars and forgers'.)
>
> Charles Peguy, *Basic Verities*, 1943, 'Lettre du Provincial', 21 December 1899

The theme of this book is the secularisation of the West and the impact of that on society. Britain is merely the most extreme example of a trend.

These essays trace the effects on ordinary people of being the first post-religious society. Every other society in every part of the world has had at its heart the existence and practice of religion.

But this book is not just a social history. It is also a guide to how we as individuals can change history. We can comment as much as we like on society but we must go on living our lives; we must grow ourselves spiritually, and put our spiritual beliefs into action.

So shall we start with ourselves? Some of these essays are written by Muslims and Jews. Islam in particular has much to teach us. Not the fanaticism of the suicide bomber which dominates the media and informs foreign policy, but the tradition of day-to-day religion for ordinary people. The Muslim prays five times a day. Religion is a fundamental part of his daily life. But although 72 per cent of the population claim to be Christian, most are virtually non-practising (only a tenth of this number goes to church on Sunday).

Islam tells us that religion cannot be an occasional add-on to life; it is fundamental to life. Daily communal worship, meditation and spiritual reading are confined to a tiny proportion of Christians. Yet it was not always so. Once, the Angelus rang out three times every day over the fields and people stopped working at noon to pray. This is brought to life in Millais' famous picture.

Is this a far-fetched notion, that a nation could re-evangelise itself? I do not know.

I do know that daily contact with a quiet period of spiritual reflection of any kind immeasurably helps health, calmness, acceptance and putting all things – most of which in reality matter little or nothing – into perspective.

Yet we are a long way from that, for most people. The modern mind craves certainty. But religion based on faith needs to be built on uncertainty. It can never be proved or unproved.

Since Newton and Descartes, Western philosophy has been cursed by the Paradigm of Certainty: if we cannot prove something scientifically, it is not truth. Christians believe in the Paradigm of Truth. That faith is rational. That God is reason. He is the laws of the universe. He can't suspend a metaphysical law such as 2+2 = 4.

But I think Christian leaders make an extraordinary error in basing so much of their teaching on the assumption that people do believe, when most are mildly agnostic or receptive in a vague sort of way to the likelihood – and no more – of a Supreme Being. I think we should all be what I call 'assumists'. Assumism accepts that religion is incapable of proof. We should throw ourselves over the precipice of uncertainty and plunge into the waters of belief. Read the Scriptures, practise them and then experience the great unfolding of joy that comes.

I wonder if 'assumism' will ever catch on? It does at least provide an escape from a nagging angst of modern life – the eternal questions 'Why?' and 'Is it true?' – which contribute so much to an underlying and rarely stated dissatisfaction and restlessness.

So the first theme of this book is the value of religion at a personal level.

The second is its value to society. Or rather, the dangers of its absence. Is it mere chance that Britain, one of the world's most secular societies, also has the worst-behaved teenagers in the world? Is it because they spend less time with their parents than elsewhere, or is it more that parents and children spend less time at prayer? Does the decline of religion have an impact on our schools, our social security, our freedom under the law, the cohesion of our family life?

If an established set of rules and a moral code is undermined, is there a result on our behaviour? The answer must surely be yes.

The third theme is that the very freedoms which Muslims, Jews and non-believers enjoy are based on the Christian tradition of tolerance that underpins our laws and institutions. But there is no reciprocity. Nowhere in the Middle East is it easy or even possible to build churches. Here Muslims are free to practise and to build.

The final theme of this book is that Christianity, and the Judaeo-Christian tradition, is the inspiration of our history, of our law, of our institutions. Forget that religious tradition and you turn your back on our past, on what made us, on who we are. We do that at our peril; but that is what we are doing. We have been doing it for far too long. It is high time to retrace our steps.

CHAPTER 1

GRAVE SYMPTOMS

EDWARD LEIGH

It is undeniable that, in the last four or five decades, there has been a massive decline in religious practice in Western Europe. The Archbishop of Canterbury says that ours is a country where 'tacit atheism prevails', adding that British society concentrates only on the 'here and now', so that considerations of eternity are 'irrelevant'.[1] One senior Anglican bishop has even said the Church of England could disappear 'within a generation or two',[2] and the head of the Catholic Church in England and Wales, Cardinal Murphy-O'Connor, has said that Christianity 'as a background to people's lives and moral decisions, and to the Government and social life of Britain, has almost been vanquished' in Britain. Christians, he thinks, must adapt to 'an alien culture'. Our society is 'one where the only good is what I want, the only rights are my own and the only life with any meaning or value is the life I want for myself'.[3]

The statistics on church attendance bear this out. The number of regular church-goers of all denominations in Great Britain has declined from six million in 1980 to a mere four million in 2005 – a fall of one third in the last quarter of a century. According to Dr Peter Brierley, the director of Christian Research, if the current rate of haemorrhage continues, the number of practising Muslims will outnumber practising Anglicans in 2013.[4] An Anglican spokesman responded by saying such comparisons 'underestimate the number of worshippers on Sunday, let alone leaving out many who worship on other days'.[5] Apart from the possibility that there are Muslims who worship on days other than Fridays, this is clutching at straws. In all parts of the country – with the exception of some pockets of evangelical and black Pentecostal resistance – church-going is in an apparently irreversible tailspin.

All the literature on church attendance over the last 50 years points, unsurprisingly enough, to the secularisation of the UK as the primary cause, although there is also evidence that fewer people nowadays belong to *any* membership organisations. Political parties have also suffered from this latter trend. But to say this is only to beg the question whether this is not in itself a symptom of secularisation, given its damaging effects on the unity of the family and hence on the sense of communal obligation. These trends have all been reinforced by the combination of the Sunday Trading Act of 1994 and, to some extent, by increased ownership of cars. Three times as many people now do their shopping on a Sunday as in the early 1980s.

These developments do not of course in themselves prevent attendance at church, but they obviously increase the number of distractions. In 1995, Michael Howard agreed to extend the licensing laws so that people would not have to wait four hours after three o'clock on a Sunday afternoon to have another drink. With many pubs showing Premier League games on satellite television, Sunday horse-racing and betting were also legalised in the same year.

So it would be irrational to deny that British religion – which, of course, means Christianity in one form or another – was in an unhealthy state. Yet in spite of a veritable cornucopia of accumulating evidence of the consequent grave damage to society, there is a self-imposed rule among politicians that for them the love of Christ is nowadays the love that dare not speak its name. As Pope Benedict said in an interview, 'In political life, it seems almost indecent to speak of God, as if it were an attack on the freedom of those who do not believe.'[6]

I know this from experience. Often when speaking in defence of some Christian principle or other – be it heterosexual marriage or the right to life of the unborn child – I have been criticised and called a variety of names. The Cornerstone Group of socially conservative Tory MPs which I helped found at Westminster in 2004 has been dubbed 'Tombstone' and called 'a joyless gang of Pharisees'[7] in the press. This is no doubt because we have had the temerity to remind people that Christianity is a founding principle of Conservatism.

The reasons for the decline of Christian practice, measured by church-going, are manifold, of course, owing something to the popularisation of the view that scientific rationalism had superseded and disproved religion, something to the spirit of rebellion made fashionable in the 1960s by the various facets of commercialised pop culture, something again to changes in the liturgies of the various churches. Or perhaps there are just many more things to do on a Sunday.

But these all boil down to one basic change in the culture of Western Europe: the exaltation of the view that it is the individual who is his own master. It is the fulfilment of the devil-worshipper Aleister Crowley's saying 'Do what thou wilt shall be the whole of the law'.[8] Or, put another way, it is the attempt by people to fulfil the Serpent's promise to Eve if she and Adam ate of the forbidden fruit: 'Ye shall be as gods, knowing good and evil'.[9]

And then there are the inevitable consequences: family breakdown, often leading to increased depression or other mental illness, and even crime and suicide. As the Judaeo-Christian tradition clearly buttresses traditional and lifelong marriage, anything that weakens its influence on people will lead to increased rates of divorce, as well as procreation by cohabiters who never bother to tie a formal knot. Remarkably, a child of cohabiting parents is 20 times more likely to be abused than that of married parents.[10]

From the Judaeo-Christian point of view, all this seems obvious, but religion or no religion, the evidence for the benefits of marriage as against the evils of divorce and cohabitation, as study after study shows, is now mountainous.

There are also the depressing statistics on abortion (some 500 a day on the NHS and more than six million in nearly 40 years since legalisation),[11] child abuse (an average of one child killed each week by their parent or carer),[12] crime (much of it drug-fuelled or drug-related), alcoholism (the alcohol-related death rate nearly doubled from 1991 to 2004),[13] drug abuse, obesity (one in six children was obese in 2002)[14] and so on. We are killing our children in the womb legally at an unprecedented rate – and, increasingly, raping and sometimes killing them out of it (over a quarter of all rapes recorded by the police are committed against children under 16 years of age); we are producing an ever-increasing number of disturbed young men who drift into crime, having had little or no contact with a father (70 per cent of young offenders come from single-parent homes[15]); we are drinking, drugging, eating and – through promiscuous casual sex – sleep-walking ourselves into stupor, venereal disease, infertility and early death. As T.S. Eliot wrote some 70 years ago:

> ...it seems that something has happened that has never
> happened before: though we know not just when, or
> why, or how, or where.
> Men have left GOD not for other gods, they say, but for
> no god; and this has never happened before...[16]

Christianity, although based on an intimate individual relationship with God, also imposes, as a consequence of this relationship, grave obligations of self-denial both in the vertical relationship to God and in the horizontal relationship to society: 'If you love me, keep my commandments.'[17] No wonder, then, that Christianity has become increasingly unpopular in an era when most people's behaviour seems to be based on the premise that every individual has a right to self-fulfilment, only providing he does no deliberate harm to another person (at least without that person's consent). In such a context it is possible for people to talk about 'my truth' and 'your truth', so demonstrating a re-definition of the word 'truth'.

I write as a practising Catholic – but not as a man free from doubt. Contrary to my friends' assumptions, I am not one of those whose soul overflows with religious certitude. In fact, that is the whole point of my purely personal assumist theory. It is not simply an abstract idea; it arises from my own experience of persevering in faith *in spite of* my doubts. It is a thoroughly practical, one might even say, pragmatic approach. It almost boils down to: just try acting as if it was true, and see what happens. What have you got to lose? I can only say that, for me, I have lost nothing worth having and gained immeasurably in countless ways – but that is not the same as saying I have certainty.

THE THIRD WORLD AND THE NEXT WORLD

Public statements from bishops – even Catholic bishops – in the West tend to concentrate on 'issues' such as Third World poverty, homelessness or abortion. These are, of course, vital issues for Christians, as the Gospels powerfully imply. The trouble is that solving the problems of the Third World is not the *primary* job of the Church. The Church has always understood that her primary purpose must be to reform the souls of individual men and women. As Edward Leen put it, 'The Church undertakes to change men, not systems. She knows that if men become what they ought, systems will become what they ought.'[18] Jesus said 'My kingdom is not of this world'[19] and resisted not only the temptations of Satan, but all attempts by the men of his time to enlist him as a military leader who would overthrow the unjust Roman occupation of the Holy Land and restore its kingship to Israel in his own person. It is quite clear that, had he wished to pursue the military route, he could have mounted a powerful movement of resistance. But he did not accept the contemporary version of 'liberation theology'.

If modern churchmen spoke more often and with greater force and clarity about the development of a personal spiritual life and the direct relationship with God – the essence of faith rather than the works that ought to spring from it – there might be less interest in the 'New Age' and more in the New Testament. The default faith setting of most British people, as evidenced by their generosity to such charitable events as Red Nose Day and Children in Need, is a sort of alternative religion – entirely in line, it seems to me, with the general approach of the established Church. Pelagius was a fourth-century heretical monk who believed that men could be saved by their own efforts without the help of God's grace – the extreme opposite of Luther's position. Perhaps most people are now Pelagians without ever having heard of him.

It may not be a bishop's job to formulate political policy, any more than it is a politician's job to tell people what religion they should practise; yet it is part of a politician's job, if he follows a particular faith, to stand up in public and proclaim that a religious faith of some sort is important. We should encourage religious debate and let people make a choice on the basis of what they hear. Of course, they may choose to reject the whole concept of God; but it is surely wrong to deprive them of the opportunity to consider the subject by refusing to raise the issue at all.

If, as the Church has proclaimed for 2000 years, the truths of Christianity are facts, then they are the most important facts for anyone to know. To fail to take account of their implications, or to refuse to debate them in the political arena, is to deprive both its practitioners and those who vote for them of vital knowledge about the philosophical foundation and framework of the principles which have informed our culture and our laws for centuries.

Our current culture is unprecedented in its attitude to politics and religion. When Tony Blair said, rather tentatively, on a television chat show that in deciding whether or not to go to war in Iraq he believed that he would be judged by God,[20] he was mocked by the Lib Dem leader Menzies Campbell, who laughingly claimed he was 'not as devout as many people, and in particular...not as devout as the Prime Minister'.[21] When asked if he had prayed at any point in the leadership contest, Menzies Campbell laughed off the question: 'I certainly didn't do that!' The very idea seemed to strike him as ridiculous. And one of his MPs, Dr Evan Harris, said Blair's comments were 'bizarre'. He warned against politicians making 'references to deity' in public life.[22]

When he made his address to the nation on the eve of the Iraq war, the Prime Minister wanted to sign off with 'God bless you'.[23] Innocuous enough, you might think; but even this not particularly fanatical sentiment was vetoed by his advisors. As Alastair Campbell famously said when shutting down another avenue of inquiry on this topic: 'We don't do God.'[24] And Jeremy Paxman's sneer was even more supercilious than usual when he mockingly asked Blair if he prayed with President Bush.[25]

So it is not surprising that politicians should be reluctant to talk about their faith in the current atmosphere. As Blair himself explained to the *Observer*, he once gave an interview in which he was asked three times if he was saying that if you are a Christian you have to vote Labour, that each time he said no, but that the headline was something like '"If you're a Christian, you have to vote Labour", says Blair'. As he commented: 'The fact is you never, ever, ever, in our politics, get into this argument and get out of it without people misconstruing it.'[26] He is absolutely right; in this area more than any other, the press treat their political interviewees as puppets. Kipling's point about 'the words you've spoken twisted by knaves to make a trap for fools' are all too apt. And above all, the secular press appears to want to make fools of politicians who profess a faith in public – unless, it often seems, they happen to be Muslims.

So those politicians willing to risk exposing ourselves to this sort of misrepresentation must do so with great care. It is important to get sound bites unmistakably clear; if they are misreported they must insist on the right to reply. But, accepting the dangers of entering this territory, they have no choice if they are to promote Judaeo-Christian values in the political sphere. To shrink from making the attempt for fear it is a vote-loser is both to miss a privileged opportunity and to fail in their duty. The current atmosphere cannot change for the better unless we make bold to challenge it. As the tide of secularisation advances, it is not enough to try to hold ground; it is time to seize it back. The alternative is simply to be swept along by the tide; it will not stand still.

What, then, is the approach we should take? There should certainly be a balance between the concerns of Right and Left, between, on the one hand, abortion, euthanasia and marriage, and, on the other, Third World poverty and human rights (the latter must of course be properly understood within the context of Christian teaching – which they are frequently invoked to contradict).

In the words of the famous Victorian convert Cardinal Newman, 'Go through the long annals of Church history, century after century, and say, was there ever a time when her bishops...forgot that they had a message to deliver to the world – not the task merely of administering spiritual consolation, or of making the sick-bed easy, or of training up good members of society, or of "serving tables" (though all this was included in their range of duty) – but specially and directly, a definite message to high and low, from the world's Maker, whether men would hear or whether they would forbear?'[27]

It almost seems, at least in Western Europe, that we are living in that time now. As the formerly Anglican canon and Catholic convert Edward Norman comments on the Church of England (he was still an Anglican at the time of writing): 'Every disagreement, in seemingly every board or committee, proceeds by avoidance of principled debate. Ordinary moral cowardice is represented as wise judgement; equivocation in the construction of compromise formulae is second nature to leaders.'[28]

One Catholic bishop, in a recent BBC interview, defended the right of Catholics to opt out of the Church's teaching on contraception: 'It's got to be a conscientious decision taken prayerfully, and all these sorts of things, and even at the end of the day if that's what they feel they have to do, then that is a decision I have got to respect.' The interviewer commented: 'The pastors of the Church in Britain understand their flock and have tended to avoid raising difficult doctrines that they know people cannot accept.'[29]

Yet if our home-grown hierarchy have ceased by and large to challenge their flock, in a historical reversal, it is now native Britons who are likely to be targeted by Christian missionaries from former colonies such as Nigeria. The Catholic Diocese of Leeds has recently appointed two Nigerian priests. The glaring difference between British and Nigerian Christianity is pointed out by one of them, Fr Kondo Vitalis: 'in Nigeria the Church is full of young people taking a very active role, while the elders are pleased to sit back and see how their legacy is being used. In the UK there are so few people coming to Mass regularly. The Church in England needs to think of new ways to get people back into churches.' He lays the blame on our wealth, and says we 'look to the government for answers and ideas instead'. He says we 'should not think government policies alone can form the moral conscience'. His remedy: 'We must follow the African example.'[30]

African clergy are doctrinally uncompromising, upholding biblical and traditional norms on marriage and sexuality. According to one report last year, 'The number of African Catholics has increased 30 per cent in a decade, to more than 130 million, served by 426 bishops and more than 27,000 priests. In Nigeria, with about 25 million Catholics in a population of about 137 million, congregations spill out onto benches outside most Catholic churches, even with five or six Masses on Sundays.'[31] The growth is attributed to a combination of population expansion and Irish missionaries proselytising in schools; African bishops, in spite of the best efforts of Western aid agencies, uphold the traditional teaching on contraception, which fits African culture.

HOW TO FILL THE PEWS AGAIN

It is clear that, over the last 40 years, none of the attempts to woo the young with folk Masses, 'raves in the nave', and so on have had a significant positive effect on the decline in church-going. Trying to attract converts by making their experience of church-going more like that of their ordinary lives and leisure activities, and by soft-pedalling on 'hard sayings', has clearly failed. To compete with the pull of the exciting variety of the modern world – as well as with Islam, which has strong attraction for some – the Church must offer an alternative of great attractive power. The offering must be presented with powerful impact, if it is to be noticed at all, in a world where many people take *The Da Vinci Code* seriously as a guide to Christianity.

There is of course no perfect or fail-safe formula. Jesus Christ himself was rejected by many of those who heard him preach. But, reading the Gospels, one cannot help notice that his reaction was never to water down his message as a result.

If, as St Paul tells us, the Church is his bride, what should she do but follow his example?

Jesus said 'I have come that they may have life – and have it to the full'[32] and 'If you hold to my teaching you are really my disciples. Then you will know the truth and the truth will set you free.'[33]

It is greatly to be pitied that, due to our failure to preach the Gospel clearly and fully, in the attributed catch-phrase of Michael Caine, 'Not many people know that'.

I believe it is necessary to call for a revival of confident public proclamation of the core beliefs of Christianity.

A faith that seems largely concerned with 'values', 'ethics', morals and political issues is like a bloodless body. Many people nowadays claim without embarrassment to be 'spiritual'. Sadly, all too few know of the spiritual riches concealed in the writings of the mystics and saints of the Church over the ages. It is high time for a rediscovery.

As Christ said to the Pharisees when they asked him to rebuke his disciples for praising him too loudly, 'I tell you, if they keep quiet, the stones will cry out!'[34]

I believe that the nations of the West are ready and waiting for a spiritual revival, but like an ember rapidly burning itself out on being taken from the fire, too many people feel they can find spirituality alone. That is very difficult for most people. It is much easier to encounter God within the loving support of a community dedicated to God. And it is easier still if that church community has a firm grip on what it believes. I say this although I am myself beset with doubt. What I like about strong evangelical and traditional Catholic churches is that the leaders seem at least to have confidence in what they believe.

I find, for instance, that if I try to follow all that the Catholic Church teaches and don't attempt to cherry-pick, both in spiritual teaching and in its moral code, a great acceptance – on occasion joy – suffuses my life. This is ironic; the Muslim and the convinced atheist think that much in Catholic teaching is illogical, absurd and based on myth. One part of me agrees. Then I throw myself off the cliff, accept it and I find joy. Could it be that it *is* true after all?

One thing I do know. Bishops must concentrate on what they and they alone can do: proclaim the vital importance of the personal quest for God. There are plenty of politicians and journalists willing and able to ponder the challenges of global warming and Third World poverty. Very, very few of them have the courtesy to mention the R-word. So we need to hear more from politicians about the value of religion; it would be difficult to hear less. And we need to hear more about God from bishops. They'll feel I'm being unfair. They preach the Gospel in their cathedrals all the time. But if they are allowed a couple of minutes on the media, they should use that precious commodity and say to people now that they cannot do without God, tempting as it is to burnish their caring credentials by talking about the environment.

CHAPTER 2

PC ALSO STANDS FOR POST-CHRISTIAN

ALEXANDER BOOT

1

The mystery of Christianity caught people unawares though they had been warned: Christ was to fulfil about 300 Biblical prophecies. But none was heeded at the time. People neither counted years in a descending order before the Nativity nor started from zero after it. Caesar did not foresee the cataclysm awaiting Rome. Tiberius was probably unaware it had occurred.

But occur it did, and the world gasped. For God was neither just a cosmic deity nor merely a man. He was both, and understanding of that was slow in coming. But when it did come, people had to express creatively their idea of God. After all, God had expressed creatively his idea of man. If the goal of life was to imitate Christ, creative self-expression had to play a big part.

Yet in the first millennium AD such self-expression was discouraged. For example, Clement of Alexandria wrote that art contravened not so much the Second Commandment as the Eighth: by displaying creativity, man was stealing God's prerogative. But towards the second millennium, things began to change, and it was through culture that Christians learned to express their understanding of God. St Anselm's definition of culture as 'faith seeking understanding' set the terms, raising culture to a status it had never enjoyed in the Hellenic world. As its importance increased, it grew more intricate, with entry restricted to fewer and fewer people.

Christianity, in its pre-Reformation shape, was esoteric too. Its universality was owed to the power of its message, but only as relayed by priests. Although vernacular Gospels always circulated in small numbers, a serious attempt to disseminate them was a burning offence in Europe as recently as the 16th century. Thus a universal religion paradoxically expressed itself through a hierarchical culture. In order to thrive, this culture had to excrete the protective cocoon of a compatible civilisation.

Western civilisation had no option but to mirror the culture's exclusivity. But culture's meat is civilisation's poison. Since the masses had numbers on their side, their exclusion could be sustained only by concentrating political, financial and military power in the same hands that moulded – if not themselves created – culture. This amounts to a definition of an aristocratic society. Whatever we may think of its fairness, it was the only arrangement able to provide the soil in which Western culture could grow and, consequently, Christianity could flourish.

This observation must be qualified as the rule of aristocracy never was undiluted, at least in England. In fact, no political arrangement can exist in its pure form without degenerating. Following Aristotle, Machiavelli argued that, when their purity is rigidly maintained, a principality turns into a tyranny, an aristocracy into an oligarchy and a democracy into an anarchy. For a political arrangement to last, a state must combine the elements of all three known forms of government. That is why the synthetic constitution of Lycurgus in Sparta outlasted the democratic constitution of Solon in Athens – and why the English constitution outlasted any of its Western counterparts.

After the Reformation, the individual became more sovereign in religion, and increasing numbers became dissatisfied with secular exclusion. They wanted to uphold their own interests which, with metaphysical culture off-limits for most, had to be materialistic. Thus the co-existence of Christian culture and civilisation could not remain peaceful forever. The potential for conflict was always there as the aristocracy could protect its cultural domain only by relying on coercion, thereby militarising its civilisation. This was more than just an oxymoron. It was the guillotine waiting to happen.

The threat to the Hellenic world came from outside. But the culture of Christendom was such that most citizens of its 'polis' were cast in the role of internal barbarians. Christendom's own Alarics were as hostile as the nemesis of Rome, but they were wrapped in an equivalent of togas, not animal skins. That is why their hostility was harder to detect, though as impossible to resist.

Hostility seethed beneath the surface, only waiting for the physical strength to catch up. The more people were excluded and the stronger they got, the more certain was the revenge, and the more sanguinary its form. Thus, paradoxically, as Christian culture grew more sublime and consequently more exclusive, Christendom became more vulnerable. But as culture was a source of Christendom's historical strength, the paradox sharpens to a razor's edge: as Christendom grew stronger, it was growing weaker. The Reformation drove this point home with shattering force.

2

The Reformation shifted the accent from ontology to epistemology by placing God into man's own existential realm, where to be or not to be became the question. To be was no longer the answer. But radical reformations of any kind are a dangerous game to play. Luther and Calvin, or Cranmer and Tyndale, should have thought twice before throwing out the baby of clerical mediation with the bathwater of clerical corruption. They should have sensed that the shock waves of such an explosion would never be attenuated.

Alas, they were unaware of the law since then amply proven: Any reform produces effects different from those intended. The likelihood of such effects turning out not just different but opposite is directly proportional to the zeal involved. The reformers introduced into Christianity both pre- and post-Christian values, thus devaluing the object of their veneration and, because of their zeal, achieving results opposite to those intended. Instead of inspiring religious revival, the Reformation paved the way for the English, American and French Revolutions.

When a man is encouraged to define his own religion, sooner or later he will become his own God. Thomas Jefferson is one example of this: some of Christianity was acceptable to him, some was not. So he clipped the acceptable passages out of the Bible and pasted them into a notebook, creating his own Scripture. One can argue that most Protestants go through the same exercise in their minds, if not literally. Atheism is the logical if unintended long-term result, even when it is masked by fulsome protestations of piety.

The blows that rained on Christendom as a result of the Reformation also struck against the secular fabric of society. For example, the nature of geopolitics changed as France and Holland or England and Spain had acquired a divisive difference that could not be settled by nuptial arrangements. From then on, European countries were no longer just Christian. They became either Catholic or Protestant, and their churches had to take political sides. This rendered unto God that which was Caesar's, compromising both.

By demystifying the Church, the Reformation made it vulnerable to anticlericalism. The thunderous anti-Church broadsides of Luther and Zwingli were custom-made for the sombre Germanic countries. In France wit worked better. This is why, in the two-odd centuries before the head of Louis XVI plopped into a wicker basket, the personage of a venal and lustful monk, priest or nun was ever-present in French literature, from Rabelais to Molière to Diderot. So when we read these writers' works, we should remember they are not just brilliant bagatelles. They are Iago whispering into Othello's ear.

3

The Enlightenment shunted God aside as the eschatological dynamic, leaving man himself as the only candidate to fill the vacancy so formed. Descartes' *cogito, ergo sum* set the scene nicely: 'I' was the new 'He'. This shift was not so difficult to effect since the dominant philosophical doctrines had already made God more or less redundant.

If anticlericalism was the practice of barbarian onslaught, deism was the theory. While anticlericalism relegated priests to an antiquarian status, neo-Gnostic deism demoted God himself to part-time employment as some kind of demiurge. To a deist, God may have lived but is now dead. Admit grudgingly that he may have created the world, grant him no further role in life, and there is no need for ranting off soapboxes. Just wait for atheism to take over.

The wait will not be long: agnosticism comes out of deism the way Eve came out of Adam's rib, and then atheism is just round the corner. Agnosticism is deism plus logic; atheism is agnosticism plus politics. Characteristically, Voltaire and Rousseau, who rival Marx and Darwin as the patron saints of atheism, were themselves not atheists but deists. They did not mind paying occasional lip service to God while demolishing his house.

England lent them a helping hand. Locke, Hobbes and then Hume pushed empiricism to the forefront of public discourse. Locke in particular became perhaps the most popular philosopher in the 18th century. The embryonic PC man was attached to Locke: divine inspiration was no longer seen as an essential cognitive tool, which was welcome news to those devoid of such inspiration. Knowledge was what emerged once the facts obtained by the senses had been processed by reason. The world was knowable only empirically. Man needed to look no further than himself as the repository of knowledge.

Linked to humanism was its political extension: liberalism. Empiricism and liberalism were a combination made in secular heaven. If people were now independent of God, it followed that they should also be independent of lesser authority, within reason. Equality before God now had to be replaced with social, political and economic levelling. This may have been merely a theoretical deduction by Locke, the longing of a statist PC man in the making. But hindsight tells us that Christendom was to find the fruits of liberalism poisonous.

Hume's trust in empirical knowledge was just as strong as Locke's. No wonder he became the darling of Paris salons and Rousseau's good friend: Hume's French admirers were lifting man to the pedestal previously occupied by God, and empiricism was a sturdy winch. Man no longer needed a deity for any practical purpose; he was becoming both autonomous and sovereign.

The same trend is observable in science: until the 18th century, most scientists were believers who used science to get closer to God by learning more about his creation. Once science was torn away from its theological underpinnings, scientists turned away from God. As they believed reason knew no bounds, now it had been untethered by the *philosophes*, they could see their way clear to using science to prove that God did not exist.

The French, told to doubt everything by Descartes, were now prepared to go further along that route than had been fathomable hitherto. They were not quite happy with Hume who, dissatisfied with both the *a priori* and *a posteriori* proofs of God's existence, presaged Kant by inferring that the existence of God could be neither proved nor disproved by reason. The illogical conclusion Hume drew from this inference was that *ergo* God does not exist: he was an atheist after all. But his was not the atheism of his French chums – it lacked the fervour springing not so much from disbelief in God as from belief in the opposite of God. Even though Hume denied faith, he still did not go so far as to pass atheism as irrefutable fact. This was lily-livered as far as his politicised friends were concerned. They wanted Hume to go one better.

4

By acclaiming the sovereignty of the individual, the *philosophes* shoplifted the ethos of Christianity. In the Judaeo-Christian tradition, the importance of the individual derived from the grandeur of God. Prostrate humility before the latter was a precondition for the proud self-assertion of the former. The *philosophes* snipped off the connecting links, casting God adrift and dragging such concepts as freedom and love into the new secular domain. The individual was now to feel proud not of being created in the image of God, but of his own autonomous self. This closed the loop of the vicious circle inside people's minds, and their heads swelled.

The internal barbarian liked what he heard. For centuries he had been taught that he ought to spend his whole life atoning for original sin. Now he was told that was nonsense: he was good to begin with, and further perfectible. For Christ, original sin was something to redeem. For Rousseau, it was something to dismiss. While before people had to toil to become good, now they could devote the same energy to becoming happy, while others would take care of perfecting them. No effort was required on their part. Happiness, proclaimed by the *philosophes* and enshrined in the American Declaration of Independence, ousted virtue as the aim of life.

But what exactly was happiness? Rousseau and some *philosophes* had a ready answer. They reminded people how in the unlamented past they had been equal only before God. Now it had all changed: we are born equal not only in that narrow sense, but in every respect. At birth we all resemble the primitive man – *noble sauvage*. That chap felt unabashedly happy tossing his hirsute female onto the grass. And he was good, not having yet been exposed to the corrupting influence of Christendom. Moreover, he was equal to other noble savages in wealth and social status. Alas, that good individual was destroyed by those with a vested interest in his subjugation: kings, aristocrats, priests.

The conclusion had to be clear. Let us get rid of these leeches and return man to his happy-equal state socially and politically, while still enabling him to acquire the trappings of modern wealth. Equality was thus portrayed as both a desirable and an achievable objective, and Fichte was to write that promoting it was the only true function of the state.

5

As people were both perfect and tautologically perfectible, it followed that they were all qualified to govern themselves by electing the worthiest among them to attend to the actual business of governing. It also followed that any other form of government was anathema, as it would block the paths leading from private goodness to public virtue.

When these ideas were first put into practice, Frenchmen were handed liberty on a platter. But upon closer examination, this piece of proverbial chinaware was instead found to contain a pile of severed heads. First, the ruling class had to be democratically brought down a peg. Then the merchants had to be democratically dispossessed. Then the clergy had to have their property democratically confiscated. Then the army officers had to be democratically cashiered. Then the farmers had to have their crops democratically requisitioned. And then they all met under the democratic guillotine.

That device went into high gear and ran up a score never before even approached by any state not listing secular brotherhood among its desiderata. The only people set free in the process were the rabble: free to murder, rape and plunder. The newly elected tool of the people's power had to conscript the mob into the National Guard, so as to gain some control over it and to counterbalance the old army that inclined towards scepticism about *liberté, egalité* and *fraternité*. Overnight the country's army tripled in size, and France fell under military control.

The new state realised Rousseau's ideal: 'The state should be capable of transforming every individual into part of the greater whole...; of altering man's constitution for the purpose of strengthening it. [It should be able] to take from the man his own resources and give him instead new ones alien to him and incapable of being made use of without the help of others. The more completely these inherited resources are annihilated, the greater and more lasting are those which he acquires.'

Every modern state created since, be it liberal or totalitarian, has had this ideal burnt into what Durkheim called its 'collective soul'. Only the tactics changed from one to another.

6

Residual resistance to modern vandalism had two basic patterns to it, followed with minor deviations everywhere. The French pattern represented a principled stand based on a sense of rectitude. French aristocrats espoused the traditional view of their role, and would never see it as an unbilled walk-on. They did not want compromise; their disdain for the internal barbarian was too deeply ingrained. That is why PC men turned against them armed not only with egalitarianism, but also with passion. PC men no longer just wanted them out. They wanted them dead.

In England, tradition had learned to resist in a cleverer way, and so it could be ousted only by attrition, not frontal assault. The English constitution, evolving over a millennium, had balanced the interests of every estate. It thus gave the English a tool for reaching a compromise at a time when one of the estates, the common man, was no longer prepared to accept the traditional equilibrium. But compromise can be a perilous affair. As Burke's exegesis showed so powerfully, the English constitution embraced every liberal tenet, in the Lockean sense. What Burke did not mention was the kiss of death following that embrace.

For no marriage is possible between Christendom and the internal barbarian. Social compromise is useful for preventing social upheaval. It bribes the internal barbarian into abandoning his murderous instincts and agreeing to win in a non-violent way. But it cannot prevent his victory. Thus, though England has more or less managed to avoid the physical destruction of Christianity within her borders, she could not prevent its fading into the background.

Burke also failed to realise that the American Revolution he extolled had come from the same philosophical source and pursued – albeit by different means – the same goals as the French Revolution he decried. Both revolutions were perpetrated by the new species: PC man. However, two different sub-species were involved: the philistine, who begat the liberal version of the PC state; and the nihilist, responsible for the totalitarian variant.

But neither the nihilist nor the philistine exists in an undiluted form. They cohabit in the breast of a PC man. Given his natural inclination and outer circumstances, one of them can at times assume a greater importance, but not to the point of ousting the other. Thus even the most bloody-minded nihilist can still pursue material 'happiness', whereas the most complacent of philistines will still harbour violent feelings towards tradition. That is why modernity cannot co-exist with Christendom any more than a rap song can fit into a Shakespeare sonnet. '*Shall I compare thee to a summer's day and then carve thee up, thou bitch*' does not quite ring possible.

7

With the nihilist storm brewing on the continent, England assumed the role of pathfinder for the philistine sub-species. Even as the agnostic empiricism of Locke and Hume had provided the philosophical basis for PC man's first tentative steps, the utilitarianism of Bentham and Mill now propelled him to the bauble of the Industrial Revolution.

Bentham followed Hume as inexorably as Marx followed Bentham, what with Christianity disappearing from philosophical equations. Bentham and Mill eschewed Hume's honest but ill-advised attempts to find a basis for absolute morality outside faith. In doing so they abandoned absolute morality. For, unchecked by the eternal and immutable arbiter, morality can only be relative, which is to say nonexistent. Rather than a house able to withstand any storm, it can only be a weather vane sensitive to the way the wind is blowing. Man may have an innate moral law within him, as Aristotle and Kant believed. But if so, this law is suspiciously flexible: the secular view on what is moral changes from one age to the next, from one society to another and even from one individual to another. Add and multiply all those changes, and Kant's moral law begins to look more like an expedient than an imperative.

Instead of the Christian polarity of virtue and sin, the utilitarians postulated the PC polarity of happiness and pain as the starting point of moral choice. Happiness was good and therefore virtuous. Pain was bad and therefore sinful. The morality of a choice had to be judged by its outcome. If a choice led to happiness, it was moral; if it produced pain, it was not. A century later Hemingway expressed this concept with his typical crudeness: if something feels good, it is moral.

Using this logic, one has to believe that Fred and Rosemary West were paragons of morality, as their murderous peccadilloes undoubtedly made them feel good.

Though the complexities of Christianity were now in the public domain, their accessibility was of no use to internal barbarians. They had no time for complicated things; their time could be spent more profitably on pursuing happiness. So Bentham and Mill made sense to them. 'The greatest happiness of the greatest number' was a licence to destroy traditional culture, which had been produced for a few by fewer still. With numbers working for them, PC men were ready to tighten the screws, creating what Tocqueville called 'the tyranny of the majority'.

Once absolute standards of good and evil were tarred by the brush of relativism, the numbers game began to be played in the arena of morals and aesthetics, areas not hitherto available for mass pageantry. Politics and economics had to follow suit and, in the year Bentham died, the Reform Act inaugurated the political ascent of modernity in Britain.

Since the greatest happiness of the greatest number was now seen as utilitarian and therefore moral, it followed that the greatest number should have a direct impact on their own political happiness. This meant that franchise had to expand *ad infinitum*. The extent of its expansion was no longer dictated by Burkean prudence, but rather by the utilitarian expedient of how much PC men could get away with at any given time.

8

By the 19th century all the destructive weapons of PC modernity were in mass production. But they needed sharpening by radicalism. This came from the economic determinism of Marx and the biological determinism of Darwin, later abetted by the psychological determinism of Freud.

Marx's materialistic picture of life as an ongoing clash of hostile classes, each striving to expand its economic bailiwick at the others' expense, has served both sub-species of PC man well. For example, even if they reject Marxist economics, most Britons today accept the class view of life as a given – in spite of a Tory prime minister extolling classless society, the multimillionaire Alan Sugar calling himself working class, and Tony Blair trying to master the glottal stop.

But whatever service Marx provided for the philistines was unintended. It was the nihilists who gained most from his theories, as Marx gave them something they had been missing: an eschatology to fit their instincts. Assault on Christendom could now be put on an intellectual footing. While the kingdom in heaven had already been debunked beyond a comeback, the kingdom on earth was at last described in detail. For Marx outdid Moore and Owen by creating a utopia that did not look utopian. His ideal society appeared to be there for the taking.

The popular view is that Marx's ideals are worthy but unachievable, or else that Marx's theory was perverted by Soviet practice. In fact, Marx's ideals are unachievable precisely because they are so evil that even the Soviets never quite managed to realise them fully, and not for lack of trying. Where the Bolsheviks perverted Marxism, they did so in the direction of softening it.

Abolition of all private property, militarisation of all labour, turning all women into communal property and all children into wards of the state remained a sweet dream. Bolshevism only came close to realising the Marxist dicta by hatching what Engels described as 'special guarded places' to contain aristocrats, intelligentsia, clergy and other 'harmful insects', in Lenin's phrase. Such places have since acquired a name, but in essence they are exactly what Marx envisaged. However, Lenin and Stalin were again found wanting in spreading concentration camps to a mere half of the world.

Not only has every attempt to implement Marxism failed to make people free, it has also failed to make them equally rich – or even equally poor. Yet, though the fallacy of Marxism has been demonstrated, the rumours of its demise are exaggerated. For Marxism answers PC men's need to find a justification for their hatred of tradition. So they will remain forever grateful, no matter how many academics now advance their careers by abandoning Marxism, and no matter how many Marxist states now use 'ex' as their first name. Marxism has been widespread not because its home was in Russia, but because it is in PC man's heart.

Darwin became another pilot of modernity by steering biology towards Bentham and Marx. Reducing man to his physicality rang mellifluous PC bells. Yet any honest observation of life reveals an incontrovertible fact: an animal man may be, but he is not just an animal. Describing him as such misses the only point worth making: man's mind and soul, his unique metaphysical self. And though there is evidence of physical evolution, none exists of any incremental development in that faculty.

Fossil evidence shows practically instant transition from beast to man; the earliest sites of man's habitation show him to be as intelligent as most scientists, and more artistic. This punches a hole in Darwin's theory, with all those endless atavisms he cherishes. An aeroplane resembles a tricycle in that both are made of metal, have three wheels and can transport people. However, anyone who offers this explanation to a visiting Martian, without mentioning that aeroplanes fly, is not partly right or almost right. He is either mendacious or mad.

Darwin repeated Leibnitz's fallacy of nature knowing no leaps, of everything having developed gradually. His contemporaries doubted that theory. Our contemporaries reject it outright. *The Descent of Man* now holds more than curiosity value only for the stridently politicised. Terms like 'big bang', 'intelligent design' and 'irreducible complexity' are now used not by theologians, but by biochemists and geneticists. Many inch towards Genesis in their view of creation. Few accept that an amoeba can evolve into a human being, even one as flawed as Richard Dawkins.

9

The Reformation encouraged every man to fashion his own God, for the Church could not be trusted. The Enlightenment taught him to be his own God, for the original one was dead.

Darwinism told him he had better be his own God, for there never had been any other. And Marxism said the state was God, with proletarians its angels.

These doctrines formed PC man; each subsequent doctrine was formed by him. Most of them were embellishments on the formative ones, or else their pale imitations. For example, the logical positivism of A. J. Ayer was but an attempt to modernise Hume. The Frankfurters Marcuse and Adorno fell out of Marxist buns. Post-modernism and deconstructionism merely put a modern twist on the antinomian relativism of the Enlightenment. The likes of Dawkins and Wolpert try to put the moth-eaten Darwinian straitjacket on life. Of the modern prophets only Freud cannot be traced back to an antecedent, which goes to show that originality is not a redeeming quality by itself.

Much as they extol reason, PC people are not about thought. They are men of action. Their idea of the world is fully formed; they may welcome new suggestions, but they do not really need them. The formative doctrines gave them their marching orders and march they did, mostly to man foxholes and firing squads. While ripping the heart out of Christendom, the 'progressive' 20th century produced between 300 and 500 million victims – more than the previous recorded history combined.

To make sure that others would follow, PC men had to relay the marching orders in a language to which others would respond. As there was no more absolute truth in their world, there could be no more absolute meaning in their words. This had to be relative, communicating whatever suited PC men's purposes at the moment. For language stopped being a conveyor of meaning; it became a mechanism of power.

Lewis Carroll realised this before anyone else, which is why Humpty Dumpty conducted this dialogue with Alice: 'When I use a word', Humpty Dumpty said in rather a scornful tone, 'it means just what I choose it to mean – neither more nor less'. 'The question is', said Alice, 'whether you can make words mean different things'. 'The question is', said Humpty Dumpty, 'which is to be master – that's all'.

The nihilist 'master' rules by the gun – therefore he must have a monopoly on the use of guns. The philistine Humpty Dumpty rules by the word – therefore he must have a monopoly on the use of words. If he chooses to describe as 'free' a healthcare system that costs at least 10 per cent of people's income, then that is the meaning he will enforce. If he wants people to believe – or rather not to enunciate disbelief – that racial murder is morally worse than any other, or that an even spread of illiteracy is comprehensive education, or that homosexual marriage is as commendable as the old kind, he will use force to ensure compliance.

This becomes a test of power, and it works only when people are made to use words in other than their true meaning. That is why Karl Popper was too timid when saying that, for an idea to be true, it has to be falsifiable. (Famously, his statement that an idea is either tautological or open to empirical proof is itself neither.) More in keeping with PC, Kant would be saying that, for a modern idea to be true, it has to be false.

Thus both meanings of PC, post-Christian and politically correct, morph into one gaping whole. Christianity, the sublime mystery which made everything else limpid, has been replaced by atheistic solipsism, which makes everything else murky. And so the modern world limps along, waiting for God to prove yet again that, just as there is death implicit in life, so there is life implicit in death. That, though Christendom appears dead, it can rise again as it has done many times in the past.

CHAPTER 3

MAKE YOUR OWN HOPE

PETER MULLEN

European civilisation and culture – and even our very existence – are under threat from two ideological enemies: militant Islam and an equally militant internal process of secularisation. Professor Marcello Pera is a philosopher and President of the Italian Senate, and in his book *Without Roots* he writes:

> Is there a war perhaps? I answer yes there is a war and I believe the responsible thing to do is to recognise it and to say so regardless of whether the politically correct thing to do is to keep our mouths shut.
>
> In Afghanistan, Kashmir, Chechnya, Dagestan, Ossetia, the Philippines, Saudi Arabia, the Sudan, Bosnia, Kosovo, the Palestinian Territories, Egypt, Morocco and much of the Islamic and Arab world, large groups of fundamentalists, radicals, extremists – the Taliban, Al Qaeda, Hezbollah, Hamas, the Muslim Brothers, Islamic Jihad, the Islamic Armed Group and many more – have declared a holy war *jihad* on the West. This is not my imagination. It is a message they have proclaimed, written, communicated, preached and circulated in black and white. Why should we not take note of it?

In fact, we prefer not to notice it and so we are dying of political correctness.

The Muslim religion has expanded by military conquest from its very beginnings. If Charles Martell had not defeated the armies of the Caliphate at Tours in 732, Europe would have become an Islamic province. In 1095, Pope Urban II preached the first crusade at the Council of Clermont and summoned all Europe to wrest the Holy Lands back from the Turks. Sultan Mehmed II captured Constantinople by force in 1453 and ended the Roman Empire.

In Malta in 1565 there was a notable confrontation. The Muslims were besieging the island and they captured and killed some of the Christian Knights of St John. Suleyman the Magnificent beheaded them and floated them across the harbour on crosses. The Grand Master of the Knights of St John, Jean Parisot de la Valette, cut off the heads of many Turkish prisoners and fired them back at the enemy like cannon balls. Gosh – whatever would the General Synod say?

Six years after this, 197 ships of the Muslim fleet were destroyed by Don John of Austria at Lepanto and the Muslim insurgency was diminished. It was at the height of the Reformation, yet Catholics and Protestants were briefly united in thanksgiving for what was definitely seen as a marvellous deliverance. In 1683, Muslim imperialists were at the gates of Vienna. The repeated pattern of history for more than 1000 years reveals periods of aggression by Islam leading to conflict with Christian Europe, resulting in interludes of Islamic retreat and retrenchment.

We are at the beginning of a further period of Islamic expansion today. In November 2006 the head of MI5 announced that the agency was investigating 30 ongoing terrorist plots in Britain and keeping under surveillance as many as 1600 suspects. She added that the war on terror would last for another 20 years. But it has lasted intermittently for 1400 years and at present it is mounting a renewed assault.

Islam is a militant faith. From the start, Muslims believed in expansion by conquest. Efraim Karsh's recent book *Islamic Imperialism* describes this policy in detail and he quotes the Founder Mohammad:

> "Fight all men until they say there is no God but Allah."
> As Charles Moore has pointed out, "Osama bin Laden

quoted those words immediately after the attacks on the twin towers."

The British press and the BBC continually upbraid European nations for their history of conquest and 'imperialism', but make no criticism of Islamic imperialism. And while the slave trade, along with 'Hitler', is a favourite topic in schools' history syllabus, there is rarely mentioned the fact that the biggest slave traders of all were in fact the Muslims and that their operations were brought to an end by the British navy. Heathen Africans counted as less than human for the Muslims. British colonial rule actually replaced the Muslim slave trade in Africa. Muslims are bad minorities in any country, continuing their violence against Hindus in India and Buddhists in Thailand.

We are, however, constantly being told that the Muslim civilisation of the Middle Ages was a superior thing – an influence so benign that it actually helped Christian thought to prosper. The Islamists claim the medieval philosopher Averroes as one of the bright lights of Islamic history, and indeed he was – a man who understood Aristotle and rescued him for modernity. But Islam persecuted Averroes for his thought, his writing, his deeds; so it is ironic that the successors of his persecutors now claim him as their pride and joy. Maimonides was a Jewish contemporary of Averroes and as great a man, a philosopher and doctor. He was given the choice of death or exile by the Islamic rulers of Spain – those Muslim conquerors of Spain who, pro-Islamist writers like to say, were so extraordinarily tolerant!

As Moore says in his review of Karsh's book:

> Islam provided Muslim leaders not only with a justification for violence, but also with a permanent excuse. They can always blame things on the infidels. Arab nations have again and again avoided helping the Palestinians or coming to terms with Israel, because the settlement of that issue would turn the focus on their

own failings. Hamas explicitly rejects a Palestinian state, preferring the pan-Arab state that can never be.

In his book *What Went Wrong? The Clash between Islam and Modernity in the Middle East*, Bernard Lewis sums up the impediments to peaceful co-existence and says that these derive from the fact that Muslim states never developed industrially, so they have for 300 years pathologically envied the West. They have no science, no democracy, no women's rights and, apart from oil, no exports. So they do not enjoy the ameliorative and co-operative effects of lively free trade.

Lewis also cites what he calls 'the blame game' – blaming the West for all the ills of contemporary Muslim states:

> For the governments, at once oppressive and ineffectual, that rule much of the Middle East, this game serves a useful, indeed an essential purpose – to explain the poverty they have failed to alleviate and to justify the tyranny they have intensified.

Lewis concludes:

> If the peoples of the Middle East continue on their present path, the suicide bomber may become a metaphor for the whole region and there will be no escape from the downward spiral of hate and spite, rage and self-pity, poverty and oppression.

The stand-off between Islam and the West has been intensified mightily by President Ahmadinejad of Iran. This man is not an ordinarily ambitious politician. He is a sincere religious fanatic who believes that it is his duty to provoke a conflict with the enemies of Islam – us – so that the supernatural figure, the Hidden Twelfth Imam, will return to earth as the Mahdi for a final decisive showdown with the forces of evil. Again, that's us. Nothing short of Armageddon. When Ahmadinejad addressed the United Nations last September, these were his closing words:

> O mighty Lord, I pray to you to hasten the emergence of your last repository, the Promised One, that perfect and pure human being, the one that will fill this world with justice and peace.

Niall Ferguson, writing in May 2006, implored us: 'Are we doomed to grasp the consequences of all this only when the mushroom clouds are rising over Tel Aviv and Teheran?'

I wonder if even that would be enough to rouse the West from its torpor. I was in Oxford at a church conference on 9/11. Twenty or 30 clergy, we all gathered in the common room and watched the atrocity unfolding on the big screen. Over in a corner one priest was orchestrating pacifism. Another said in my ear, 'I hope Bush doesn't retaliate'. I said, 'I hope and pray he does!'

I got straight on a train back to London. Your head is full of terrible thoughts and apprehensions at such a time. And I recall the banner headline in the *Daily Telegraph*: AMERICA AT WAR. And I thought there might be just one consolation for the appalling events in New York. I almost said aloud to myself: 'Well, at least that's the end of political-correctness.' I thought at last spades would be called spades and there would be an awakening to reality.

And for a few days it seemed like it. People were strangely quiet in the City as they went about their business. There were no airliners over London. There were more people at the weekday Masses and more coming into church to pray by themselves. I put on at two days' notice a Requiem in St Sepulchre's and more than 200 turned up: City workers, silent, awe-struck – not a mobile phone went off in the whole hour. I made no concession to sentimentality and gush, but made the service out of the Latin rite and *The Book of Common Prayer*. When they left church many were in tears. A week later and all this had worn off. The atmosphere reverted to its usual unconcern and studied triviality.

It is said that when God retreats, Allah advances. God has certainly retreated throughout the last 200 years in western consciousness. And so the other equally lethal threat faced by the West is home-grown secularisation. Militant secularists and atheists such as Richard Dawkins operate a ruthlessly reductive pseudo-scientific ideology which claims that human beings are nothing but genetic information glued on to bits of protein and proceeding entirely according to Neo-Darwinian determinism. Religion is a primitive delusion – even a 'virus'. The universe might look as if it had been designed but, say the secularists, this too is a delusion. There is no mind behind the creation. The universe 'just is'.

The moral and social consequences of this ideology are predictably horrific. Since human beings – so called – are nothing but bits of genetic material, they can be experimented upon, have their parts transplanted, their embryos and DNA manipulated and frozen as if by the machinations of a latter-day Frankenstein. Their very existence may be terminated when this existence is discovered to be inconvenient to the hedonistic careers of those who make up our society of utilitarian materialists – what F. R. Leavis called our 'technological-Benthamite culture'. The most disgraceful example of this nihilistic amoralism is of course abortion on demand, abortion used as a form of contraception, resulting in 200,000 embryos being ripped untimely from the womb every year in Britain alone.

Christian theology is no longer taught in the universities. Oh, I know many universities have departments of theology – but what goes on in them is not Christian. University theology – believe me, I've had plenty – takes its cue from debunking and demythologising 19th- and 20th-century German professors, and latterly lunatic Gallic influences such as the incoherent Jacques Derrida and the vile Michel Foucault.

It may surprise you to learn that teaching Christianity in state schools is now illegal. It is permitted only to teach *about* religions. Absolute relativism rules OK. All religions must be taught as equal. The only perspective from which you can teach such equality is atheism. Christianity used to be at the centre of public life and it was strongly represented in the mass media, particularly in broadcasting. What we have now on the BBC is only a veneer of religion glossing over a soft-left political agenda – secular social conscience, as if there could be such a thing – a whiff of Third-Worldism; the aroma of Fair Trade coffee and the infallible dogma of global warming.

Ours is the culture which devout Muslims rightly despise as morally bankrupt. We are in no fit state to present an alternative to the religious certainties and moral confidence of vigorous contemporary Islam. It is as if they are telling us to accept their morality, their standards. And we reply that we have standards of our own. And when they enquire of us as to what these standards are, we say in effect, 'Promiscuity to the extent of casual sexual relationships among any number of people, regardless of their sexual orientation; drinking and shopping 24/7; rampant hedonism pursuing all that is merely trivial; an infantile and narcissistic cult of celebrities – and all built on a mountain of government and personal debt and an amnesiac culture of designer drugs and oblivion.' We have replaced morality by lifestyle. Anything goes. The one remaining commandment left to us is 'Wear a condom!'

Actually, the intellectual argument against secularism, materialism and all forms of reductionism, including Dawkins' extremely crass and uneducated variety, has been won. I will set out the plain reasoning, but then I shall have to raise a further matter which does not at all appeal to the present age – not even to those who are pleased to regard themselves as being in general sympathy with traditional Christianity.

Let me begin with a question: what did you have for breakfast this morning? This is not a joke but actually a question involving profound issues in philosophical theology, and I shall return to it. Many people have been talking to me about the argument over whether the world was designed or whether it all came about through accidental processes over a very long period of time.

In modern times there has arisen this notion that religion and science are at odds – as if science were all a matter of hard facts and religion just soft faith. There are a few things to be said against this. First, a great number of scientists are religious. Secondly, it is only very recently that there has seemed to be a conflict between science and religion. If you are looking for evidence of intelligent design – that the world was made by a designer, God – then it is best to go to the modern scientists themselves.

Physicists, for instance, tell us that the whole universe operates according to the workings of four forces: the strong nuclear force; the weak nuclear force; the electromagnetic force; and the force of gravity. If any one of these forces had been minutely stronger or weaker, no material universe – let alone life – could exist. Dr Gerald Schroeder, a leading physicist at the Weizmann Institute, tells us what modern science says about the nature of the physical universe:

> The world we see as solid is made solid not by matter but by ethereal forces carried in photons – themselves a theoretical construct – travelling immense distances between the nuclei and surrounding electron clouds. The world of atoms and molecules consists of wavelike particles separated from each other by voids, held in place by never seen massless photons, travelling at the speed of light among particles that are not only particles but also waves. If you can conceptualise this mêlée in an intelligible way, I have an urgent suggestion: Publish!

Modern physics thus reveals to us a world which does not look at all as if it's made of bits and pieces of matter, but is really rather ethereal. Less as if it's material stuff. More as if it's mind stuff. Moreover, it looks overwhelmingly as if the universe was made with us in mind, for, if it had been ever so minutely different, we wouldn't be here. The odds against the universe happening by accident to be so accommodating to us are so astronomical as to be virtually impossible. And, note, it is not theologians who are making this point, but scientists. They have even coined a phrase to refer to the hospitableness of the universe: they call it 'The Anthropic Principle' – because the world seems to have been constructed with man in mind. Dawkins and his school might reflect on the fact that we are able to understand at least a little of the universe only because the universe is intelligible. It is the innate intelligibility of the universe which makes science possible. That intelligibility was not created by man or imposed on the universe – at least that much must be conceded if science itself is to be regarded as a way of discovering truth, and not merely a game.

In a vivid sentence, Professor Fred Hoyle said, 'Life evolving by chance has the same likelihood as a tornado blowing through a scrap yard and leaving behind it a fully-formed jumbo jet.'

Well, what do determined atheists make of all this? They reply by suggesting that there is not one universe, but an infinite number of universes. And given an infinite number of universes, there was always going to be one just right for us. What an improbable conjecture to fall back on! It's as if I should play a game of heads or tails with you and every time you won demand we toss the coin again. And it is not a new device. St Augustine came across it 1600 years ago and dismissed it as '...the Epicurean fantasy of innumerable worlds'.

Why do we always imagine our controversies are so original? William of Occam, writing in the 14th century, warned '*Entia non sunt multiplicanda praeter necessitatem*' – in other words, 'Don't artificially imagine more things than you need.'

The Neo-Darwinian fundamentalist Richard Dawkins says, 'Just because something looks as if it was designed doesn't mean it was in fact designed.' I would turn his dogma the other way round and say, 'We know there is design in the world – because we ourselves design things. And it is entirely implausible that our idea of design could have arisen in a world that was chaos, undersigned.'

Dawkins believes that all we are is genetic information glued on to bits of protein. Really, is that all we are? Let me prove here and now that this is false. And let me do so by returning to that deep philosophical question, 'What did you have for breakfast this morning?' Suppose you answer, 'I had protein, carbohydrate and fat.' And I say, 'Oh come off it, what did you really have?' And you admit, 'Oh all right – I had eggs, bacon and fried bread.'

Dawkins – with his 'We are nothing but our genes' – is like the man who won't believe we had eggs, bacon and fried bread, but insists all we had were protein, carbohydrates and fat. Or to give another example, Dawkins is like a man who went to a symphony concert and you asked him what he heard. And he replied, 'Oh sound waves in different frequencies.' When you tell him that's a damn silly answer, he is of course shamed into admitting that what he really heard were Beethoven's Fifth and Shostakovich's Tenth.

Neo-Darwinian fundamentalists, materialists and bad logicians such as Dawkins actually refute their own argument. Dawkins says, 'We are only our genes.' I tell him he's wrong. He himself is not only his genes. He is his interest in biology, his relationship with his wife Lalla Ward (who was once Dr Who's delightful companion). He is all his hobbies and pastimes – perhaps his love of music and painting, his enjoyment of a game of chess and his irrational hatred of religion.

The world cannot be reduced to mechanism and materials. And the sane man never does describe the world in purely mechanistic terms. If you do describe the world only in terms of genes and molecules, of material bits and pieces, you are not describing the real world. For you are leaving out the whole realm and variety of human experience – including incidentally the study of science.

But there is a deeper issue here. When we come to ponder these great matters about the origin and purpose of the world, what is our perspective? Where do we stand? The philosopher René Descartes famously asked, 'Is there any knowledge so certain that no reasonable man can doubt it?' And his answer – his absolute presupposition – was his own existence: 'I think, therefore I am.' In other words, he thought his own existence more certain than the existence of God.

Wittgenstein said that in order for Descartes' proposition 'I think, therefore I am' to be basic, Descartes would have to own the language in which he spoke the words. It would, after all, be a bit of a giveaway to insist on the primacy of your own existence but then to make the claim in language you admitted you'd learnt from other people! What other people? The philosopher Antony Flew tells a nice anecdote featuring Wittgenstein at the Moral Science Club in Cambridge in 1949 for a lecture on Descartes. The speaker stood up and said, '*Cogito ergo sum*', whereupon Wittgenstein said in a loud stage whisper, 'That's a bloody stupid place to start!'

The idea that my existence is more certain than the existence of God is so preposterous that only an atheist could believe it. And once again there is nothing new in this nonsense. Six hundred years before the birth of Christ, the prophet Jeremiah satirised the hubris of man's supposed self-sufficiency. Jeremiah said that the clay is in no position to question the being of the potter: 'Saith the Lord, as the clay is in the potter's hand, so are ye in my hand.'

When Genesis and St John's Gospel tell us that in the beginning was the Word of God, they are telling us the truth that our words – including our scientific words – have meaning only because they are derived from the Eternal Word. We cannot stand, as it were, alone in empty space and ask 'Does anything mean anything?' If the question about meaning is itself meaningful, it must be because there *is* meaning already. This is not unscientific. It is why theology was called 'The Queen of Sciences'. In God we live and move and have our being.

It's one thing to win the intellectual argument against secularism and atheism, but it's a much more difficult thing to live out the truth of Christianity in public life. As Kierkegaard said, 'It's one thing to be able to stand on one leg to prove the existence of God, but quite a different thing to go down on your knees and thank him.' The task is the restoration of Christian England. This is the one thing which can save us from both the threat from militant Islam and the amorality of contemporary culture and society.

There is some enthusiasm for doing this, but the enthusiasts misfire. Even those sympathetic towards the attempt to restore Christian values hardly dare bring themselves to believe it can be achieved. Even so profound and subtle a thinker as Roger Scruton reckons that traditional Christianity cannot be restored in Europe. Many agree with him. They think we can achieve some sort of revival of civic religion as a way of underpinning our efforts at trying to be good. Christianity may not be true, they say, but it can be jolly useful for a conservative moral and political programme. But what's the point basing any programme on something that is not true? It is all rather reminiscent of Voltaire who despised religion but thought it good for crowd control – 'for the servants'.

It won't work. As long ago as 1934 in *Choruses from the Rock*, T. S. Eliot asked:

> Do you need to be told that even such modest attainments
> As you can boast in the way of polite society
> Will hardly survive the faith to which they owe their
> significance?

In other words for Europe, for England, if Christianity goes, then everything worthwhile goes with it. For:

> There is no life that is not in community
> And no community not lived in praise of God.

Ethics needs transcendence. There is no morality without God. When we try to invent a morality without God, we end up only

> ...dreaming of systems so perfect that no one will need to be good.

The current expression of this folly is of course political correctness, health and safety, anti-racism, anti-sexism, anti-ageism (and all the other antis) glued on to a secular interpretation of human rights. As if we were trying to re-run the French Revolution, only this time, in true Pelagian fashion, hoping to manage it without the guillotine.

But Eliot had a word of hope. He asked us to consider:

> Do you need to be told that whatever has been can still be?

Christianity has not been disproved. It is not a primitive delusion, one of the childish things that we have put away. As Chesterton said:

> An imbecile habit has arisen in modern controversy of saying that such and such a creed can be held in one age but cannot be held in another. Some dogma, we are told, was credible in the twelfth century, but it is not credible in the twentieth. You might as well say that a certain philosophy can be believed on Mondays, but cannot be believed on Tuesdays.

Almost worse than rejecting the faith and becoming an atheist is this bizarre attempt to employ Christianity in the pursuit of quite another programme – as if civic morality or conservative politics were some sort of higher good. All such attempts in fact treat Christianity as if it were a metaphor for something else. Whereas what is required is to believe the faith and embrace it with all one's heart, mind, soul and strength. We must recover our sense of devotion and our practice of the faith.

The people of the Bible, Jews and Christians, have been in this predicament many times. And always the cry of the prophets is to call the people back to God:

> In returning and rest shall ye be saved: in quietness and confidence shall be your strength: but ye would not. (Isaiah 30:15)

> Rend your heart and not your garments, and turn unto the Lord your God: for he is gracious and merciful, slow to anger, and repenteth him of the evil. (Joel 2:13)

> If we say we have no sin, we deceive ourselves and the truth is not in us. But if we confess our sins, he is faithful and just to forgive us all our sins and to cleanse us from all unrighteousness. (John 1:8–9)

It is possible for people to return to God – they did so sincerely but only briefly when I put on that Requiem Mass after 9/11. It does not reflect well perhaps on human nature when we witness again just how fickle we are and how we turn to God only when we are afraid. But that is the way it is. The grace in it is that God will accept us even under these conditions. But, I repeat, Christianity is not a metaphor. And God is not an image of some higher good, or some externalised image of our highest interiority – as the Jungians vainly believed. There is no substitute for getting down on our knees and worshipping him.

This business of men 'dreaming of systems so perfect that no one will need to be good' usually means that we become infatuated with fantastic projects such as saving the planet – or at least saving all Africa – eradicating child poverty and such like, while ignoring the problems at our own front door. But if a man cannot redeem his own neighbourhood which he hath seen, how can he redeem Africa which he hath not seen? Our fundamental flaw is that we don't understand that we are fundamentally flawed. We think we are more virtuous than we are and that nothing within ourselves impedes us from realising in fact what are merely utopian fantasies. If I may quote from one of my own verses from some years ago:

> See the Archbishop rising from the table,
> And after lunch at The Athenaeum
> He will convene an ecclesiastical commission
> For the late repudiation of Original Sin.

It can't be done. So if we are to have hope it must be for something within our ambit. It must first of all be local. I know it can be done because I have watched as it was done in one parish. Eight years ago the parish of St Michael's in the City of

London was moribund. There were four people in the congregation for the Sunday Choral Mass. A very small number of people determined to do something about this death-in-life.

They produced an easy-to-follow service book containing the traditional form of the Anglican Holy Communion – on the lines of the 1928 revision of *The Book of Common Prayer (1662)* with the Prayer of Oblation following Cranmer's Consecration Prayer. They eschewed all casual, extraneous verbiage – the exaltation of the tautology to the level of a divine principle – of the 'It's nice to welcome you all here this morning. Let us now confess our sins in the words from the Confession on page seven of the little white book etc *ad nauseam...*' We started at the start and we went on to the end. We let the liturgy be the liturgy.

We provided sound doctrinal sermons which imagined the faith and set it out – not in terms of something else. We let the classic doctrines speak for themselves. We did not think we had to apologise for Christian teaching as they do on 'Thought for the Day', where they regard the doctrines (when they regard them at all) as only more or less useful images for highlighting social policy. Taking St Augustine as our spiritual guide, we practised believing until we discovered that we *did* believe. None of our preachers dumbed-down or patronised the congregation. After the service we met in the vestry or the garden for wine and conversation. We published books of sermons and theological reflections.

We made our programme and all our publications available on our website. We studied what it is to pray and we prayed. In a fairly short time we numbered more than 50 each Sunday – and that in a parish in the middle of the City of London, a parish with no resident population. It can fairly be said that St Michael's is now an informed, devout and affectionate company of souls.

There are other parishes which are doing the same or similar. High church or Low is of less importance than the consistent effort to present the phenomena of Christianity, and to regard the Real Presence as real indeed and not just another metaphor – for what: 'sharing' or Fair Trade coffee perhaps?

If you think that jibe is also something of an exaggeration, consider Richard Harries, Bishop of Oxford, who said we must stop using the expression, according to Our Lord's command, *This is my Body...this is my Blood* – '...or else visitors will think we're cannibals'. I am not making this up. No one could, so far has the contemporary Church of England descended into bathos. What can be achieved in one place can be achieved on the national scale. It is probably the case that things will have to get a lot worse before they get better. As we have noticed, people return to God when they are in trouble. And trouble is certainly on the near horizon. Islamic terrorists have not refrained from attacking us with biological or even nuclear weapons as if they were having second thoughts and being merciful, but only because they have so far been thwarted. But the terrorist atrocities will increase in frequency and severity.

It is surely not a pleasant prospect to reflect on the suffering we shall have to endure before we turn to the light. But when these things begin to come to pass we shall at least know once again what our religion is. It will be there in our anguish:

> Let us therefore return unto him who is the merciful receiver of all penitent sinners; assuring ourselves that he is ready to receive us and most willing to pardon us, if we come unto him with faithful repentance; if we submit ourselves unto him and from henceforth walk in his ways; if we will take his easy yoke and light burden upon us, to follow him in lowliness, patience and charity, and be ordered by the governance of his Holy Spirit; seeking always his glory and serving him duly in our vocation with thanksgiving.
> From The Commination Service for Ash Wednesday, *The Book of Common Prayer (1662)*

> Why art thou so heavy, O my soul: and why art thou so disquieted within me? O put thy trust in God: for I will yet give him thanks, which is the help of my countenance and my God. (Psalm 43:5–6)

CHAPTER 4

THINKING AND ACTING MORALLY

BISHOP MICHAEL NAZIR-ALI

'If a thing is worth doing, it is worth doing badly,' said G. K. Chesterton, and it is in that spirit I have approached this subject, recognising its importance and complexity, but also my modest ability in tackling it.

In our rapidly changing world not only are we faced with moral choices more frequently, the choices before us are increasingly complex. At the same time, there is a tendency to 'populism', that is to say to the view that what is morally acceptable in a given society must be determined by public opinion even if the reasons for holding such views are not terribly strong. On the other hand, there are influential sections of the community who stand to gain commercially or in other ways and who wish to promote a particular technology or way of viewing the human person, society as such or the world at large. In such a situation, if we are to hold our own we need to be clear about the basis for our thinking and acting morally.

In this article, we shall consider the nature of moral decisions and the scope of morality, whether it can be held to be universal, but also look at what could be specific to a culture or a time. We shall look at the relationship between natural law and revelation, as found in the Anglican tradition, and ask whether knowledge of what is naturally right can be attained naturally. In light of this tradition, we shall consider some sharp moral questions as they arise today, particularly in the field of reproductive medicine, euthanasia and medical ethics generally. Finally we shall consider, very briefly, the relationship of morality to religion and to law.

MORALITY, UNIVERSAL OR RELATIVE

First of all, in moral decision-making, we need to ask *how* we arrive at particular moral decisions. It is important here to emphasise the place of both reflection and deliberation in the process. Reflection is primarily thought about who we are and what the world is, while deliberation is, as the term suggests, a 'weighing up' of choices regarding how we should act, based on our reflection of how things are and how they ought to be. From this emerge the so-called generic moral rules, e.g. 'All killing is wrong'. Such rules may be more or less specific, depending on the extent of our reflection and the scope of circumstances we have in mind, e.g. 'All killing is wrong except in the cause of defending the weak from aggression'. However specific such rules may be, they are not particular moral judgements. In themselves these latter are spontaneous acts of recognition that a particular way of behaving is wrong, but they need, of course, to be informed by reflective and deliberative moral reasoning which has led to the framing of moral rules. A particular moral judgement, therefore, may take the form '*this* killing is wrong because it is an instance of the kind of thing we meant when we said "All killing is wrong except in the cause of defending the weak from aggression".'

While particular judgements are, of course, related to specific situations, moral rules are universal in scope. To say 'All killing is wrong', even when the rule is modified by exceptions, is obviously to make a statement that is supposed to be true of all times and all places. Such universality of moral rules is, naturally, incompatible with radical moral relativism which denies that there are fundamental moral rules which, in principle, apply to all human beings and all human societies. It may, however, be compatible with a *cultural* relativism which holds, for example, that people are not to be blamed if they act according to their conscience, in the light of cultural values, or if cultural circumstances are such that a moral rule applies in a particular way in that culture. Thus in a polygamous society a man who behaves honourably towards his wives should not be accused of offending against the dignity of women. Also, in such a society the application of the rule about the equality of women may have to be applied differently, at least for a time. History is full of examples of zealous efforts by missionaries and others to impose instant monogamy on traditionally polygamous societies with disastrous results, not least for the women themselves. It may be that equality of opportunity in education and employment, participation in political life and equality in law will bring about the desired results without such precipitate action. Ultimately, of course, recognition of the dignity and equality of women will lead to an acknowledgement of monogamy as fundamental to an adequate anthropology.

Any outright denial, however, of the universal scope of morality would leave unexplained the very general agreement among human societies, for instance, about murder, lying, stealing and betrayal. In a rapidly shrinking and 'globalising' world, where people from different cultural and religious backgrounds daily rub shoulders, moral agreement is of crucial importance. Hans Küng has pioneered the search for a global ethic and has related it closely to his work on dialogue between the different religions of the world. For him, not only peace but justice and the protection of the created order depend on this dialogue and the common ethical values which will arise from it.[1] Even a polemical and polarising writer like the political scientist Samuel Huntington recognises that people of all civilisations need to identify common values, institutions and practices. Only then will a universal civilisation emerge.[2]

It is clear that questions about human dignity and of respect for the environment, so fundamental to the identification of common values, cannot be answered on a purely utilitarian or consequentialist basis, but must take account of the nature of humanity and of the world as well as of our sense of duty, regardless of consequences, in these matters.

A UNIVERSAL MORAL ORDER?

It is fundamental to Christian faith that decisions are moral because they respond to the reality which confronts us and, above all, to the ultimate reality of God himself. 'Teleological order' in creation is of immediate significance to us if we are to understand creation and to act in relation to it.[3] The unity and 'purposed' character of the universe, of which we are part and in which we are agents, lies behind the Christian 'Natural Law' tradition which is itself grounded in the 'Eternal Law' of God's will and wisdom. If creation as a whole, and creatures within it, have been created in particular ways and for certain ends, this implies that we as agents will have to behave in such a manner as to respect this teleological character of the created order, ourselves included. Nor need such 'ends' be seen as fixed and immutable (a common objection to teleology). As James Ward saw, teleology can be understood as that purposiveness in creatures which leads them to develop 'epigenetically', achieving ends in keeping with their nature but not predetermined from the outset.[4] The scientific method of observation, abstraction and discovery of new relationships between objects is not in itself inimical to teleology. In fact, teleology may be an ally if it posits regularity in nature and also helps in the integration of the sciences into a coherent world-view.

Considerations such as these have led to the view that a universal moral order is embedded in universal structures of human interaction with the world and in social interaction. This is shown, for example, in the way different cultures show respect for the environment and in the acknowledgement of the need for social structures which will promote justice. Such a view about a universal moral order does not deny the need for moral development in individuals, whether in terms of the internalisation of ideals or through learned behaviour. Nor does it deny the need to move from heteronomy to autonomy and from there to a social morality of mutual care and connectedness. In fact, if there is a universal moral order it is necessary for both individuals and society to develop in increasing recognition of its claims.

Christians affirm, therefore, the original goodness of creation and perceive an order in it which displays the wisdom of the Creator. While human ignorance, wilfulness and rebellion obscure something of the order in nature and in society, there continues to be some common recognition of good and bad, right and wrong, virtue and vice in otherwise widely diverse human societies. On the one hand, the universalisability of moral principles is both embedded in and leads to the recognition of a common moral order, and, on the other hand, particular institutions, such as marriage and the family, are universally recognised as vital for social survival, even if they have been misunderstood and abused in practice.[5]

Some moral theologians, whilst acknowledging the authority of the natural order, hold, nevertheless, that such an authority is not merely a matter of discovery but must rely on God's revelation, especially in Jesus Christ, if it is to make a full impact on our understanding and conduct. Even if this is so, we must allow some natural discernment of such an authority and some such discernment in the various religious traditions, if any project for a global ethic is to get off the ground. At the same time, we can agree that the recognition of such authority receives its definitiveness from God's revelation in Christ.[6]

ANGLICAN MORAL TRADITION

Anglican moral theology, in particular, has seen the sources of moral decision-making in the access which human reason has to Natural Law as a manifestation of the Eternal Law of God's own being and also in the divine positive law revealed in the Bible, without which sinful humans could not fulfil God's will for them.[7] The two sources are not, however, discrete and unconnected. The divine positive law affirms, corrects, confirms and clarifies what we know already of the world's teleological structures and the demands of a universal moral order. It is a guide in the necessary development of conscience and, indeed, in the correction of an erroneous conscience. Our contemporary tendency to respect conscience is entirely laudable, but such respect cannot be at the expense of that social and ecological flourishing which comes only from a recognition of and an acting upon those moral principles that are derived from the 'deep structures' of the universe and of human society. Early Anglican moralists had a tendency to emphasise the seriousness of moral obligation in terms of both social responsibility and the individual believer's path to holiness of life. In this endeavour, we are to be guided by both Natural Law and the positive divine law so that we may safely attain to life eternal.

STEWARDSHIP AND CREATION

The discernment of law and order in the universe (which is, after all, what makes science possible) should not, however, lead to the so-called naturalistic (or empirical) fallacy, that is, deriving 'ought' from 'is'. Although the world is ordered, it is not perfect, and while human societies have laws, they can also be characterised by injustice, tyranny and a lack of compassion. Whatever the circumstances, we should attempt to do our duty rather than succumb to them or try to tailor our duty to them. This would, indeed, be a sign of moral weakness. Some religious traditions, moreover, see the role of humans as exercising 'dominion' or 'stewardship' over creation. That implies, of course, that it is not to be left exactly as we find it, but that we can alter it for the greater good of humanity and, perhaps, creation itself. In the Judaeo-Christian tradition such a view is rooted in the first chapter of the Book of Genesis, where man and woman are created together in the image (*selem*) of God. The significance of such language is that it was used for the image of rulers in places where they could not be personally present. In the same way, humans are God's visible emblems or representatives on earth.[8] In strikingly similar language, the Qur'an speaks of human beings as God's representatives (*khalifah*) on earth (2.30). Both the Bible and the Qur'an, moreover, see human beings as creative in producing conditions of life suitable for themselves. In both Islam and Christianity, a 'Promethean' motif emerges which sees humanity as 'improving' on God's creation itself. Muhammad Iqbal's famous Persian work, the *Payām-i-Mashriq* (Message of the East), puts it in this way:

> You made the night, and I the lamp
> You the clay and I the cup,
> You, desert, mountain-peak, and vale,
> I, flower-bed, park and orchard,

> I, who grind a mirror out of stone,
> Who brew from poison, honey-drink.[9]

In the dialogue, the deity has accused humans of destroying the original goodness of creation and of ecological and social irresponsibility. This is the human reply to the divine charge. Interestingly it does not deny that there has been environmental and social damage, but points, rather, to what has been achieved by humanity in very adverse conditions.

Iqbal's mentor at Cambridge, James Ward, sums up Christian thinking in this area thus:

> ...this metamorphosis of nature by human art and industry, though it exceeds the wildest dreams of Fairyland, is yet throughout natural in so far as no new forces or elements are involved in its several processes and products, and the laws of nature are everywhere observed and obeyed. Yet we know that it is throughout the work of men, not the work of nature, in the sense of requiring ceaseless guidance and control.[10]

HOW FAR SHOULD WE GO?

Our own situation is, however, vastly different from the world of Ward and Iqbal. The question now is not so much whether we should seek to 'improve' on nature, but how far we should go. The identification of our genetic make-up and of particular genes which may cause or predispose certain people to disease is, perhaps, uncontroversial, especially when these people can be helped either through direct medical intervention or through counselling about life-style. Interference with the genetic structure of plants and animals without taking into account wider ecological factors is more problematic. The development of sophisticated reproductive medicine, moreover, has made it possible for the characteristics of offspring to be more and more minutely specified. This immediately raises the spectre of eugenics. To put it at its sharpest, are children ends in themselves or merely the means of parents enjoying yet another product of our technological age? Similar issues arise, for example, with xenotransplantation: should animals be produced solely for this purpose and made to live in quarantine for the whole of their lives? What is the risk of transmitting new viruses to human individuals and communities? To what extent is it permissible to use treatment which requires high levels of immuno-suppressive drugs and life-long monitoring? Are there alternatives, such as growing tissue from the patient, for certain kinds of treatment?

Developments in technology, emphasis on autonomy and the value given to 'public opinion' have all conspired to raise particularly acute questions about the beginning and end of life. It is generally agreed that human gametes, while living human material, are not accorded any specific status in terms of the sanctity of life. Is there then a human person at the moment of conception, when the gametes come together, or is 'personhood' something which develops as the embryo is embedded in the womb, grows into a foetus and is, eventually, born into a community? Christian tradition has, for a long time, distinguished between the 'formed' and the 'unformed' foetus (based on the Septuagintal translation of Ex 21:22). This allowed a distinction between the abortion of a formed foetus, which was regarded as homicide, and that of an unformed foetus, which was seen as sinful but not as homicidal.[11]

RESPECT AND PERSONHOOD

Such distinctions also allowed the later development of ideas of 'ensoulment'. For St Thomas Aquinas, for example, this occurred at about 40 days after conception (Aquinas also distinguished between male and female, and the time it takes for the respective ensoulment of each, but that is not relevant for our present purposes). He saw ensoulment as the emergence of organisational and directional principles in the foetus. It is interesting that this is also, approximately, the time when scientists expect to see the establishment of a functioning nerve net and the beginning of brain activity. In law, it appears that the foetus begins to be treated as an individual person when it is deemed capable of extra-uterine survival. As technology develops, this period changes, standing at the moment at 22–24 weeks of gestation.

Clearly there are watersheds in the long journey to birth: conception, implantation, the beginning of brain activity, viability outside the womb, all of these are important and have led some to take the view that we must remain agnostic about the precise time that we have a human person. This should, however, lead to *increased* respect for the embryo and foetus, as we do not know when personhood commences.[12]

The 1990 Human Fertilisation and Embryology Act's limit, then, on embryonic research to 14 days or until the appearance of 'the primitive streak' (when the cells that form the foetus separate from those that form the placenta), whichever is sooner, may be regarded as conservative. Before this, the developing embryo is not distinct and the possibility of identical twins, for instance, cannot be discounted. For some, however, even such a conservative limit is not conservative enough. They would reject the view that because there is considerable natural wastage in the earlier stages of gestation, there can be little harm in using for research material much of which would be discarded anyway. They would argue also that the deliberate creation of embryos for research is quite different from natural wastage. Even if the early embryo is not fully a human person, it has the potential of becoming one and should, therefore, be treated with respect. From the Christian point of view, the Bible certainly speaks of the foetus in personal terms, and even as capable of being filled with the Holy Spirit, but it is not clear at what stage of development this might be or even if the language is really about God's future purpose for the person to be born, rather than present reality (Ps 139:13–16, Jer 1:5, Lk 1:15, 39–45, Gal 1:15).

RESPECT FOR THE DYING AND THE DEAD

At the other end of life, there is a host of sharp questions about 'the right to die', the role of medical practitioners in assisting death and the question of 'non-voluntary' euthanasia, where the patient is not competent to give consent. The patient's right to die is an argument based largely on grounds of personal autonomy. While those grounds appear attractive to some, there are particularly difficult problems associated with this argument: how far in advance should a decision not to have treatment be made? If it is made too far in advance, it will not be able to specify the conditions under which 'a living will' is to be put into effect. If, however, such a decision is made at a time of great distress, when a terminal illness is diagnosed for example, can it be regarded as 'reasonable'? How should we evaluate the role of relatives and even of the State in encouraging people to end their lives if looking after them is going to be an increasing emotional and financial burden?

If we affirm that the role of medical practitioners is 'not to kill' but that neither is it 'to keep officiously alive', what is 'officious' in the circumstances? Is it not to withdraw uncomfortable, even painful, treatment when it is known that such treatment cannot help the patient? Is it to abstain from providing pain-killing drugs because they may cause death earlier (the so-called secondary effect), or is it to continue with nutrition when the practitioner knows there is no hope of the patient ever regaining consciousness? Michael Manner identifies the two opposite kinds of abuse in relation to terminally ill patients: benign neglect arising from a denial of the patient's condition; or, on the other hand, overtreatment which can be painful, humiliating and unnecessary. He advocates the 'good death' of the hospice movement, where the patient is as free of pain as possible and is provided with a high quality of life.[13] There *does* seem a distinction between providing treatment judged necessary to relieve pain, which *may* bring about death, and the deliberate administration of drugs to *cause* death, or even the withdrawal of nutrition and hydration *knowing* that death will result.

Much support for modern practices of euthanasia seems to be the result of the widespread view that terminal illness and serious pain go together and that the medical world needlessly prolongs life. I understand, however, that contemporary medicine can free most terminal patients of serious pain and that it does not encourage the unnecessary prolongation of life.

Another difficult issue has to do with the 'harvesting of organs' of brain dead persons who have either given prior consent or whose relatives have given consent. Published surveys show consistently that people are sympathetic to the use of their organs after death and that relatives usually respect the wishes of the deceased in this matter. They also show, however, unease about 'presumed consent', that is, people having actively to opt out if they do not wish their organs to be used after death. Various ways have been suggested of removing this unease, including giving relatives the right to object if they wish to do so.[14]

Respect for the dead is an important principle which involves some recognition of the continuity between the deceased person and the body. Such a body, at burial or cremation, should be, recognisably, the body of the person who has died. Any harvesting of organs should not be such as to violate this continuity or to cause unnecessary distress to the mourners.

Being clear about the point of death is also of crucial significance. If 'brain stem death' is generally accepted as such a point, we must be clear that this involves the irreversible loss of capacity for bodily integration, cognition and sentience. Moral theologians, of different views, have often warned about the dangers of pronouncing death too quickly and of moving the body with undue haste, especially when the use of organs is on the agenda.

In certain cases, individuals who are brain dead are kept 'alive' through mechanical and medical means so that their organs may not deteriorate before they are removed for transplantation. Questions have been raised as to whether 'elective ventilation' means that the point of death has been postponed. If so, is it moral, indeed legal, to harvest organs while, for example, the heart is beating? The process can also involve a 'stripping' of the body's parts. Is this consistent with the principle of respect for the dead? It is true that major medical and surgical procedures are rarely without their gruesome aspects, but usually they are for the benefit of the person concerned. Elective ventilation is for the benefit of others and thus in a different category. Great care is needed, therefore, in its use and in the way bodies are treated.

At the most, organ donation can be treated as a sort of 'intermediate technology' which may be acceptable to

Christians whilst other, ethically acceptable, alternatives are being developed. From an ethical point of view, such alternatives should minimise harm and maximise respect for both the living and the dead. The generation of tissues and, eventually, organs from somatic (or 'adult') cells would certainly fulfil these conditions. If research goals for organ donation and transplantation, in addition to improving current procedures, could include the development of such alternatives this would be an advantage.

REVOLT AGAINST 'MERE' UTILITARIANISM

Because of the rapid advances in technology which we have noted, there is a temptation to argue in a crudely utilitarian way, particularly if it promotes scientific progress. If people's desires and preferences can be satisfied, through scientific means, why should they not be? Why should parents not be able to select their children's sex if they wish to 'balance' their family? Why should research on embryonic stem cells not be allowed if it is going to help people with serious diseases and, logically, why should reproductive cloning be prohibited as, for some, it may be their only chance of having a child?

It is, perhaps, true to say that we can see the beginnings of a revolt against this kind of thinking. People, like Tony Blair himself, are beginning to ask questions in terms of 'intrinsic value' rather than 'use'. It is true that some sophisticated utilitarians incorporate such ideas into their thinking, but, generally, utilitarianism is not associated with them. A transcendental basis for ethical thought and action may come to be more in demand. The end does not always justify the means and human beings, in particular, should never be treated merely as a means. The parents, for example, of a very sick child would not be justified in having another *simply* so that its organs, blood or marrow could be used for the benefit of the first. The birth of a second child may, indeed, have benefits for the first, but that should not be the main reason for its existence.

Those responsible for welfare policies are having to ask whether we should always define them in 'materialist' terms such as housing, clothing, food and even physical safety, or should, rather, our focus be on the promotion of spiritual and social values which will contribute to the welfare of societies and individuals? A debate in Parliament on football hooliganism in July 2005, for example, was dominated by demands for ensuring that ordinary football fans should be enabled to enjoy the game they had paid to watch and that the general public should be protected from drunken and extremist violence. *Basic questions about the socialisation of those who committed such crimes, their family background, what sort of education they had received and so on were scarcely touched on.*

Again, there is renewed and growing awareness of the need to 'work with the grain of nature'. This is not all obscurantism; most recognise that human civilisation is built on intervention in the course of nature and this is illustrated particularly well by the worlds of medicine and of agriculture. There is concern, however, that some procedures are not so much about enhancing productivity or the natural qualities of plants, for instance, as about alteration of their basic structure which will affect the kind of thing they are, leading to unknown and possibly widespread environmental consequences.

RELIGION AND MORALS

What is the relationship between religion and morals? We have seen already that moral awareness in relation to the world at large and, in particular, within human communities is widespread, and that the development of a common moral discourse, so crucial for our times, depends on this awareness. While such awareness is not necessarily linked to a religious world-view, historically the evidence must be overwhelming that moral discourse, if not awareness itself, is closely related to and often arises from such a world-view. The great moral codes, such as the Ten Commandments and the Sermon on the Mount, are all embedded in religious traditions. The discipline of comparative Religious Ethics, for example, provides some support for this view, even if its very possibility has been questioned by those who would deny any kind of cross-cultural rationality. Then there is the question about motivation. It is true that there have been and are individuals who are motivated towards moral behaviour without having religious beliefs. On the other hand, religious traditions often form the ground for the formation of an educated conscience which, in turn, motivates action. It can, of course, readily be granted that non-religious people can act morally, indeed altruistically, and that they may be, in some cases, morally better informed. Still, the question arises as to whether they can give an equally satisfactory account of certain moral principles: for example, the equal dignity of all human beings, the primacy of conscience and our sense of duty. As Kant saw, such an account can, perhaps, better be given by reference to a Supreme Being who is both the ground for such ideas and the one who makes them attainable, if not in this life then in the next.[15]

Religion can, therefore, not only give an account of the moral and motivate us to act in particular ways; it can provide a world-view within which moral discourse can be placed. It has been the gradual disappearance of such a world-view from our society which has led to widespread questioning of 'traditional morality' and to the sense that moral behaviour is free-standing and arbitrary, without any special relationship to ways of understanding the world and ourselves. The area of religion and morals is a large one and there is room here only to mention in outline some of the issues at stake.

MORALS AND LAW

Another question which is often asked and which has enormous significance for the future is about the relationship of morality to the law of the land. It is, of course, a truism to say that what is morally desirable is not always appropriate for legislation. There is, nevertheless, a very real connection between morals and the law. Legislation must have sound moral underpinning and law must have moral, as well as coercive, force. The two principles underlying most recent legislation are those of liberty and the prevention of harm. Both have strong spiritual and moral connotations. Liberty is deeply rooted in Christian ideas of conscience and responsibility for our actions. As far as the criterion of 'harm' is concerned, it is far from clear that this applies only to other individuals. It is, in fact, widely acknowledged that it must include harm to society and to those institutions which it needs for its survival and prosperity. These certainly include marriage, the family and the essential dignity of the human person. Thus marriage and family law will not only make sure that the 'goods' of these institutions are not harmed, but that people within them are never treated merely as a means; hence the safeguarding of monogamy and the life-long nature of marriage, even in the secular realm. It must be for reasons such as these that the European Convention on Human Rights, recently incorporated into domestic law, exempts states from or limits the application of some of its articles on grounds of morality.[16]

FINALLY

We have considered, then, how we arrive at moral decisions and the basis for them. We have looked at the ways in which morality is universal, but also at ways in which it could be relative to a particular situation or culture. We have considered, briefly, the roots of the Anglican moral tradition and whether it can be used today. We have examined some contemporary moral dilemmas, including questions about personhood in the context of the very beginnings of life and its ending. We have attempted to both relate morals to religion and law and to make necessary distinctions between them. Finally, we have asked how we can give an *account* of moral awareness and behaviour, and have sought to do this in terms of our response to the reality which confronts us, most of all, to the reality of God himself. As Richard Hooker has said:

> the being of God is a kind of law to his own working: for that perfection which God is, giveth perfection to that he doth.

CHAPTER 5

QUO VADIS?

ROGER SCRUTON

[This chapter is the text of a speech delivered at the Catholic University of Milan, June 2006, first published in *Il Foglio*, June 2006]

A little chapel on the *Via Appia Antica* reminds us of our fate. There it was, according to the legend, that St Peter, fleeing persecution by the Roman authorities, was arrested in his flight by the figure of Jesus, appearing as from nowhere. '*Domine, quo vadis?*' he asked, 'My Lord, where are you going?' And Christ pointed the question back at him, so that Peter knew what he must do. He returned to Rome and his mission.

The question is today in all our hearts: 'Where are we going?' Europe seems to be fleeing from its past, from its inheritance, from its Christian mission. And yet it is fleeing to nowhere. The great European project, which is supposed to justify all the social, legal and political changes that are being imposed on us, has suddenly revealed its emptiness. Politicians have thrust this project upon us by trickery and deception. The nation states of Europe, they told us, will remain free and democratic. We intend only a coming together of friends, an exchange of commerce and a promotion of common interests. And little by little the bureaucracy has grown, our legislative powers have been stolen from us, and national loyalties have been cast aside and trampled on. For what end? Look at the proposed European Constitution and you will see. Nowhere does it refer to the religion of Europe, to the glories and achievements of the European past or to the high culture of our continent. Page upon page of empty jargon, expressing veiled hostility to the nation-state, a broadly socialist agenda, and a systematic confiscation of legislative powers. Nothing is clear in this document apart from what it denies. The document is a systematic repudiation of the European past.

Now the French and the Dutch voted against this Constitution. But it doesn't follow that it will be rejected. The European project is like the Bolshevik project of 1917: it has no 'Plan B'. The machine has been set in motion and, when it is derailed, the engineers simply put it back on the tracks. Sometimes the politicians speak of a 'slow track' and a 'fast track' into the future. But they are tracks in the same direction – namely, nowhere.

In this talk I want to describe another project: the project which ends not in nowhere but in somewhere. I believe in Europe as a place where we and our ancestors settled, in which we built great systems of law, government and religion. And I want to revitalise the Europe that I love, and find the way to be true to its mission. I don't doubt the difficulty of the task, and I shall begin by outlining the principal obstacles to a coherent European future.

The first obstacle is immigration – and the wrong sort of immigration. This problem is in the back of everyone's minds. But it is also a problem that is hard to discuss. A kind of well-meaning censorship prevails among the European elites, which permits them to refer to the social and cultural effects of immigration only by way of endorsing immigrant communities and criticising their hosts. Every suggestion that immigrants must adapt to the majority culture is dismissed as a sign of intolerance, chauvinism or racism. Yet it is obvious that there is a distinction between immigrants who wish to adapt and those who cannot or will not, and that a society that welcomes the first is quite within its rights to reject the second.

The second obstacle is connected, and that is Islam. We don't need reminding, now, that the Islamic view of the modern world is very different from the view that we have inherited in Europe. But we have yet to come to terms with the reality, or to form a coherent policy for the future. Here is the problem, as I see it. Europe is a Christian creation, indelibly marked by a faith that may be dwindling in our hearts, but which is still alive in our laws. St Paul, who turned the self-denying religion of Christ into an organised form of worship, was a Roman citizen, versed in the law. He shaped the early church as a universal citizen, entitled to the protection of the secular and imperial powers, but with no claim to displace those powers as the source of legal order. This corresponds to Christ's own vision in the parable of the tribute money: 'Render therefore to Caesar the things that are Caesar's; and unto God the things that are God's.'

As a result Christianity has always recognised the business of governing human society to be a human business, and the Christian as both a servant of God and a citizen of the secular order. The Enlightenment conception of the citizen, as joined in a free social contract with his neighbours under a tolerant and secular rule of law, derives directly from the Christian legacy. Thanks to this legacy we see political action not as a means to achieve the kingdom of God on earth, but as a way of maintaining equilibrium between people who share a home but who may not share a religion, and whose conflicts can be resolved through a common national loyalty and a common territorial law.

This contrasts radically with the vision set before us in the Koran, according to which sovereignty rests with God and his Prophet, and legal order is founded in divine command. When Islam first spread across the Middle East and the Southern Mediterranean, it was not by preaching and conversion in the Christian manner, but by conquest. The conquered people were given the choice: believe or die. Exceptions were made for the 'people of the Book' (Christians, Jews and Zoroastrians), who could enjoy the subordinate status of *dhimmi* – i.e. protected by treaty. But the treaty offered no right to worship, and forbade all attempts to convert. Other religions existed within the *dar al-islam* (the House of Submission) on sufferance, and religious toleration was regarded as a regrettable expedient, rather than a political virtue.

Much history has elapsed since those times, and in many parts of the world forms of accommodation between Muslim and non-Muslim have achieved lasting stability. Nevertheless, the old belligerence is never far from the surface. And nowhere is this more apparent than in the Middle East, where precarious regimes, constantly threatened by an upsurge of religious enthusiasm, do their utmost to paint themselves in colours that would appear favourable in the eyes of Islamic militants.

The multicultural propaganda from our elites has done us a great disservice, in making us hesitate to affirm our own precious and much fought-for secular culture, or to support those brave teachers and community leaders who have recognised that Muslims must be brought to abandon their apartness, and join in the common enterprise of citizenship. For our freedoms, rights and tolerant customs all depend, in the last analysis, on a law that is defined in national, rather than religious, terms. In a nation state people can agree to differ; they can agree equal rights for all religions; they can allow their opponents to speak their minds and influence the political process. But where religion and family are the dominant forms of social membership, despotism is also the political norm, as in the Middle East today. That is why 70 per cent of the world's refugees are Muslims, fleeing from states where their religion is the official creed, and why all of them are fleeing to the West.

Arriving here, however, bringing with them a precious legacy of family duties and puritanical values, and witnessing the licentious conduct which is the inevitable consequence of Western freedom, they often 'retreat into the shade of the Koran', as the radical Islamist Sayyid Qutb expressed it. The mesmerising verses of the Holy Book invoke a pure and untainted community, living by the law of God alone. This nostalgic vision inspires young people to turn away from reality, to refuse to accommodate or even to perceive the facts that refute it. And it generates an endlessly renewable anger against those who live by another and more easy-going code. This is the mood that has made Islamic democracy all but impossible. And it is a mood shared by many second- and third-generation Muslims in Europe who, like the murderer of Theo Van Gogh, regard the whole idea of secular jurisdiction as an affront.

Many children of Muslims therefore adhere to customs deemed unacceptable or even criminal in our culture – forced marriage, polygamy, even honour killing – and insist on schooling their children according to Islamic traditions, even when demanding that the State should foot the bill. They attend mosques where fanatical Wahhabite clergy spit hatred of the infidel from the pulpit and teach that the punishment for apostasy is death. And they record their defiance of the surrounding order in their dress. You have witnessed the effect of their intolerance here in Italy, where a Muslim convert, himself of Scottish descent, has initiated court actions to remove the crucifix from classrooms in the public schools, on the grounds that they are offensive to the Muslim minority.

Now the correct response to that kind of protest is simple. The crucifix is a symbol of the majority religion, as holy to Christians as the Koran is to Muslims. If Muslims are offended by it, then they are free to go elsewhere – to Scotland, for example, where you will not find a crucifix in a classroom, unless it is the classroom of a private school. If minorities are entitled to affirm their identity, then so too are majorities. And if minorities wish to force the majority to privatise the symbols of its faith, then they must pay the price, which is confrontation.

Of course, that is not the response that our political elite has adopted. At every point it has preferred to *concede* territory rather than defend it, to show its toleration of minority demands, by ignoring the more softly-spoken but far more legitimate demands of the majority. In short, it has preferred appeasement to confrontation. However, if modern history tells us anything, it is that appeasement never works. It was appeasement that permitted German re-armament in the 1930s. It was appeasement that offered Hitler the territories that he needed as his industrial base. It was appeasement that nurtured first Lenin and then Stalin; and it was appeasement that enabled the Soviet Union to impose its yoke on Eastern Europe. Nothing is ever gained by appeasement, which is, by its nature, a strategy of defeat. It involves renouncing one's own interests, without securing anything in return. That is what the European elites are now doing in the face of the Islamists.

This brings me to a third problem that we in Europe are now confronting, which is yet more serious than the problem of Islam. This is the problem of our own cultural identity. The European Constitutional Treaty reminds us that a great many Europeans, not least those who have taken charge of our continent, have no real affection for European culture. They see it as a historical accident that they exist on the same continent as Dante, Shakespeare and Mozart; that they reside in cities dominated by great cathedrals; that they are protected by a rule of law derived from the Institutes of the Emperor Justinian and the common-law courts of the Saxon tribes. Instead of affirming these things as ours, and the key to our shared identity and destiny, they ask us to 'diversify', advocating a 'multicultural' approach to every issue in which culture really matters. Many are, indeed, overtly hostile to the European legacy, aggressively anti-Christian, and advocates of a 'post-modern' approach which discards all attempt at a cultural consensus.

This repudiation of the European heritage is not new. You can sense its beginnings in the Enlightenment. It was a major force among the Young Hegelians, Marx especially, and has repeatedly come to the surface in the wars and contests of the 20th century. It made itself vividly felt here in Italy in the 1960s, when a kind of obligatory Marxism all but annihilated intellectual life. In those days the culture of repudiation even had a vestige of its old revolutionary fervour, with the Italian Red Brigades and the German Baader-Meinhof gang acting out a private fantasy of revenge against bourgeois society. Repudiation thereafter spread through our universities. It abandoned Marxism only to take up deconstruction, and then post-modernism – all three creeds being essentially negative, ways of rejecting the normality of European civilisation, and turning one's back on the past. From the universities the culture of repudiation spread to the schools, and now there is scarcely a public school in Europe devoted to teaching the culture and inheritance of Europe. We have a curriculum based on self-doubt, and a culture on the brink of suicide.

Well then, you will say, what are we to do? If things are as bad as you say, are we not doomed to go under, and to relinquish our continent to the Muslims? My answer is that we are not doomed, that our weaknesses are self-inflicted, and that it is by no means too late to save ourselves. The culture of repudiation provides no lasting consolation, and could be replaced at any time. And the Muslim threat will dwindle, once it is confronted, just as it dwindled after the reconquest of Andalusia and after the battle of Vienna. Nor will the insane immigration policies that have led to our current crisis survive, once we set about doing what we are now surely called to do, which is to defend our heritage.

How does this defence begin? It would be simple to call for a Christian revival, and in America such a call would no doubt attract a following. But it is impossible for Europeans to overlook the fact that their inherited faith has dwindled to a pulsation, that it is there in the buildings, art galleries and cloisters, in the literature and music of our continent, but not in the hearts of all its people. It is precisely for this reason that a new kind of movement is needed, if we are not to disappear.

When I was at university it was common to believe that we could obtain all that we needed of our Christian inheritance from culture. The morality, the spiritual discipline and the sense of community could be absorbed from Dante, Milton and T. S. Eliot. We could absorb them too from Wagner, whose *Parsifal* showed us the moral meaning of the Christian symbols, without demanding our belief in them. If we needed a philosophy there were plenty of philosophies on offer: Kant, Hegel, Schopenhauer – all of them steeped in the same Christian culture, whether or not believers in the Christian faith. I left university thinking that, if I held on to

European culture, I had the only anchor that I needed and the only anchor I could obtain, in the chaotic world of modern life.

I was assuming, like so many of my generation, that ordinary things would go on, that the unspoken assumptions on which our society rests would be upheld, and that I would find the friends, lovers, soul-mates with whom life could be shared. I was aiming for life on the rooftops, *la vie de mansard*, disregarding the fact that the rooftops have to be supplied from the ground below. As the French are now discovering, *la vie de mansard* depends on a social order in the street; and that order must be renewed if the life on the rooftops is not to lose its meaning. That, I believe, is the great task now confronting us. We cannot rescue our civilisation merely by overthrowing the Marxist, post-Marxist, deconstructionist and post-modern ideologies that inhabit the universities. Even if we returned to the classical curriculum, and taught European culture as it was taught to me, that would not bring back the public consensus on which our civilisation depends. It would simply underline the gap that exists, between our cultural inheritance and life as it is lived.

The movement that we need, therefore, is one that will revive a genuine public consensus, which will uphold the distinctive values of our culture, and which will enable us once again to will our own survival, and to will it collectively. For it is will, not prosperity, that we require, if we are to overcome the potentially fatal problems that I referred to at the beginning of this talk. In conclusion, therefore, I will suggest what kind of consensus we need to build, and how.

The most important thing on which European people can be encouraged to agree is that our inheritance is Judaeo-Christian, and that the Bible, and the two religions built on it, are an indispensable part of our culture. Even if a majority no longer believe in either the Jewish or the Christian faith, the majority can still be brought to see the importance of the tradition that unites those two, and its decisive role in the history of Europe. I believe that it is necessary to make the space, in our education system, in family life and in the public culture, for the recognition of this Judaeo-Christian inheritance. I don't mean that it should be dogmatically imposed, or that we should be constantly referring to it. I mean that it should be accorded the prominence and the honour that it deserves. And I believe that the many anti-Christian voices in our society today should be answered in kind, that a proper challenge should be presented to them, in the form of these questions: What do you want to put in its place? Will what you put in its place bring consolation? And will it give people the strength they need, to face the goals and the methods of Islamic radicalism?

Here, it seems to me, we intellectuals have some genuine work to do. The loudest anti-Christian voices are among the intellectuals, and their arguments must be addressed. One of the tasks that I have set myself is to show, as best I can, that the liberal democratic tradition which we attribute to the European Enlightenment is a Christian product. It owes something to Moses Mendelssohn, of course, the father of the Jewish Enlightenment. But it owes far more to a tradition of thinking that goes right back to the beginning of the papacy, and which recognises secular government and freedom of conscience as the two pillars of social peace. Neither of those things is recognised by the Koran, which sees all law and all government as a matter for God's regent on earth, and which allows free conversion to Islam but no free conversion in the other direction. The tension between Islam and democracy is not an accident of history. It reflects the deep opposition between Christian and Islamic views of the relation between man and God.

Now it seems to me that the secular liberties on which our cultural and intellectual life depends would not exist, but for the Christian inheritance. And they would disappear tomorrow if that inheritance were ever to be suppressed. Just look at 20th-century history for the proof. As soon as the atheist creeds of Marxism-Leninism and Nazism triumphed, all the liberties that the intellectuals treasured were extinguished. Look at the Muslim world today, where writers and thinkers are censored and sometimes threatened, like Naguib Mafouz, with death. Search for the secular liberties that we value anywhere in the world, and you are likely to find a Christian culture or a culture heavily influenced by the Judaeo-Christian tradition.

The first element in the public consensus that we need, therefore, is a habit of privileging the Judaeo-Christian inheritance. It should be privileged in debate, in the curriculum, in the universities, not so as to impose it as a faith, but so as to encourage an enlightened vision of what we are and where we are going. Young people today are starved of knowledge of this inheritance; they instinctively know that it is their birthright, and my own view is that they will embrace it as soon as it is made available to them. The conditions for this are right. For they are faced with the existential challenge of radical Islamism, the challenge which asks: What are you, that I should respect you? And no one can answer that question, who has no sense of the past.

But the work of building a consensus is not only a work for intellectuals. The best that intellectuals can do is to clear the space where ideas can flourish, and to challenge the culture of repudiation. Much more important is to reintroduce, into the culture of the people, those Christian understandings that create the social norms of the real Europe. This was the work of the Church, but the Church can no longer perform this work alone, since the Church reaches out only to a minority. Maybe European society will turn back, one day, to its ancestral faith. But we cannot assume that. More likely is a prolonged period of scepticism. Yet even from the premise of scepticism the Christian understandings can be recuperated.

We should return to the most important of Christianity's gifts to us, which is the gift of forgiveness. Happiness does not come from the pursuit of pleasure, nor is it guaranteed by freedom. It comes from renunciation: that is the great message of the Christian religion and it is the message that is conveyed by all the memorable works of our culture. It is the message that has been lost in the noise of repudiation, but which, it seems to me, can be heard once again if we devote our energies to retrieving it. And in the Christian tradition the primary act of renunciation is forgiveness – renunciation of anger and of the desire for revenge. This is something that can be taught at every level: in the family, in the classroom, in the institutions of civil society and even in the world of business.

Here I should like to make a few remarks about what Nietzsche would call the 'genealogy' of Christian forgiveness. Nietzsche saw Christianity as an expression of the 'slave morality', the morality of those whose principal social passion is not desire for success but resentment of the success of others. *Ressentiment* – as he called it – is the root, according to Nietzsche, not only of Christian humility, which is the inverted form of the desire for revenge, but also of the egalitarian and socialist ideologies of the modern world. In a virtuous society resentment would be kept in check, as the strong exert their control over the weak. In a Christian society, however, resentment is the guiding principle of the culture, and the source of the egalitarian attitudes and abject defeatism by which Nietzsche saw himself surrounded.

Max Scheler, in *Ressentiment*, his book on this topic, offers a decisive refutation of Nietzsche's critique of the Christian religion. Far from being an attempt by the weak and the cowardly to seize power over their betters, he argues, Christianity, is an attempt to confer power on everyone, through spiritual discipline and the regime of forgiveness. Resentment exists in modern societies not because of Christianity but in spite of it. The principal cause is not religion but its opposite – the obsessive fixation on the things of this world, which leads people to envy their neighbours and to seek to dispossess them. Moreover, Scheler argues, resentment is promoted by the socialist state, which is able to confiscate the rewards of successful individuals and satisfy the vengeful feelings of the failures. I am inclined to agree with Scheler, both in his critique of a certain kind of socialism, and in his exculpation of Christianity from the charge levelled by Nietzsche. But his argument only serves to underline the fundamental puzzle: why should we resent rather than rejoice in the good things that others possess?

It is a striking feature of animal behaviour that members of herds and packs do not harbour resentment, even when they fight. Once the pecking order is established, peace prevails, and all antagonism is quickly forgotten. As Konrad Lorenz argued, in his famous study, animals exhibit aggression, which has a functional role in their search for territory, but not hatred, which serves no species need (*On Aggression*, 1963). People are not like that, for the reason that their actions and motives are not determined only by the needs of species life. They also live as individual moral beings, in the shadow of judgement. Hence they can feel humiliated, worsted, degraded; they can harbour thoughts of revenge and triumph, and invest in these thoughts all the self-centred ambition of their slighted natures.

The critic and anthropologist René Girard has considered this matter in a series of striking books: *Violence and the Sacred*, *The Scapegoat*, and *Things Hidden Since the Beginning of the World*. Girard believes that violence proceeds from the 'mimetic' nature of social ties, formed by rivalry and imitation. This violence must be released from time to time, and such is the function of the scapegoat, the victim, the one who is 'cast out' and who bears the collective guilt on his shoulders. Through his death the scapegoat relieves us of pent-up anger, and allows us once again to live with our neighbours on terms. That is why he is both violently killed and, once dead, revered as a saviour. Victimisation is therefore a way in which societies establish internal peace. One function of religion is to limit the damage that this victimisation causes, by providing sacrificial surrogates, such as the animals slaughtered at the altar, or the fictional narratives of gods that die and rise again. Girard finds a kind of proof of the Christian morality in his observations, Christ being identified as the one scapegoat who was able to understand and forgive his persecutors, and therefore to establish forgiveness, rather than violence, at the heart of the social order.

Those speculations may seem wild to you, and I confess that I am not sure what to think about them. Nevertheless, there is no doubt in my mind that we rational beings are given to irrational violence, that resentment is a large part of its cause, and that typecasting and scapegoating may permit its release but may also vastly amplify its extent. (This is what we witness, indeed, in the anti-semitism of the Nazis, the anti-bourgeoisism of the communists, and the anti-Americanism of the Islamists today.) And I am inclined to agree with Girard that the Christian gospels set before us an example of the only known antidote to this potentially disastrous human failing, which is the habit of forgiving those who hate you. This antidote finds no real equivalent in the unforgiving pages of the Koran, a book that, for all its poetic inspiration and high moral tone, lacks the saving grace of irony. Kierkegaard was perhaps the first to point to irony as the virtue that united Socrates and Christ. And if I were to venture a definition of this virtue, I would describe it thus: a habit of acknowledging the otherness of everything, including oneself. Irony leads both to humility and to humour, neither of which qualities can be reliably attributed to the voice that speaks through the Koran, but both of which are abundantly present in the Gospels.

Our democratic inheritance is ultimately to be explained, in my opinion, by the radical innovation noticed by Girard, namely: the redemption offered to mankind by their own sacrificial victim, whose forgiveness brings peace. To forgive the other is to accept his otherness, and therefore to grant him, in your heart, the freedom to be. It is therefore to acknowledge the free individual as sovereign over his life, and free to do both right and wrong. A society founded on forgiveness therefore tends automatically in a democratic direction, since it is a society in which the voice of the other is heard in all decisions that affect him.

It seems to me, therefore, that forgiveness lies at the heart of our civilisation, and it is both what we have to be most proud of, and our principal means to disarm our enemies. It underlies our conception of citizenship, as founded in consent. And it is expressed in our conception of law, as a means to resolve conflicts by discovering the just solution to them. It is not often realised that this conception of law has little in common with the *shari'ah* of Islam, which is regarded as a system of commands, issued by God, and not capable of, or in need of, further justification. For us law is not a system of commands, but a system of rights, which define the positions from which we can reach agreement with each other, and so live in peace.

Those, it seems to me, are the Christian understandings that still live in our civilisation, and which need to be renewed and propagated: the rule of forgiveness, the recognition of the Other, and the belief in the Other's right to be other than me. That is what underlies the existential conflict with Islam, and that is what shows the conflict to be real. We should be proud of this aspect of our culture, and anxious to endorse it. And we should regard it as a proof of the superiority of our inheritance, even if we hesitate to go so far as the Church in arguing that it is a proof that our inheritance has come down to us from God.

In conclusion I must face the most important question to which that argument gives rise. How do you reintroduce this conception of social relations, in a world of relativism, postmodernism and radical self-indulgence? Well, not by theorising, as I have done. Theory may get you somewhere with an audience of intellectuals. But it will get you nowhere with the mass of mankind. It belongs in the *mansard*, and not in the street below.

The answer, it seems to me, was given to us by Aristotle, in his theory of virtue. We acquire virtues, he said, by imitation, copying virtuous conduct, until the motive of virtue has been engraved in the soul. The Christian understanding of society is spread not by theory but by example. And the example needs to stand out, to give a lesson not only in charity, humility and forgiveness, but in courage too. When I look at European society today I see it ready for that example; and when the example has been given, people will take heart and follow it. All of a sudden, the three problems from which I began will look like problems with solutions. People will have the will to discuss them, to address them, and to take the steps that will then be necessary, to save our continent. But one thing is certain: whoever takes the first step will not be a member of the current political elite.

CHAPTER 6

THE AMBIGUITIES OF MULTICULTURALISM

BAT YE'OR

Europeans in general think that they still have some control over their continent and over their future: control over national borders, security, justice, culture, to mention just the most obvious. Yet, during these last 30 years, goals and mechanisms have been formulated and implemented by the European Community (EC), which became the European Union (EU), without the consent or even the acknowledgement of Europeans. Political and strategic choices were imposed by decision-makers through networks spreading across all European strata, leading to the current confused situation, which projects a future of insecurity with terrorist threats from within and without, the non-integration of masses of Muslim immigrants, the feeling of a borderless Europe, and the misconceptions of multiculturalism.

Europeans think still within the framework of their historical nation-states, but this is an illusion: this framework exists no longer. Their control over territorial sovereignty and over their policy is vanishing. The Europe of nations has disappeared and it looks as if the governing body for nearly half a billion people is an oligarchy operating through networks of networks. The decision-making bodies of this entity, now comprising 27 countries, include the European Council (created in 1974), the Council of Ministers, the European Commission and the European Parliament – to name the most important. It is these top bodies that are responsible for today's grim situation.

The integration of Europe as it was conceived in the early 20th century was a positive goal. It would certainly have prevented the two world wars that have been suicidal for Europe, on both demographic and moral levels. It is this integration that makes unthinkable the prospect of an inter-European war today. And yet Europe today is a sick continent. Insecurity and fear are felt in schools, planes, trains, buses and streets. Antisemitism, hate against America and Israel are common, while its spiritual Judeo-Christian roots and universalist values are proudly rejected and denied. In other words: we share with the Arab and Muslim world a sub-culture of paranoia and obsessive hate against America and Israel. We feel that we are at war with terrorism from within and without, but our leaders tell us that we are at peace and that we have no enemies. This situation is prevalent throughout Western Europe; it results from strategic and ideological goals chosen some 30 years ago and implemented through networks without the knowledge of the European public in general. This framework encompasses the whole of the EC/EU; European countries that were outside of it were not affected.

One can distinguish here several intertwining patterns. The main one is the construction of the EU, which developed in a way opposed to the federalist conception of a 'Europe of Nations'. The European Union grew on the suppression of nationalisms and borders, and by purging European history of local nationalist and cultural prejudices. These efforts aimed to create a European multiculturalism and forge a European consciousness, culture, solidarity and a united foreign policy. The EU worked towards establishing a supra-national government that would govern half a billion people with one foreign policy, one voice that would influence world policy.

But onto this European political programme another pattern, another sister-strategy, was grafted almost immediately. This is the Euro-Arab integrative association, which duplicates Europe's integration. General Charles de Gaulle and Haj Amin Al-Husseini, the former Mufti of Jerusalem and a war criminal, conceived this strategy in the 1960s, the former acting within the European Community and the latter within the Arab League.[1]

The Mufti's ambition was to create an alliance between the Vatican, the Catholic world and the Arabs against the Protestants, the Zionists and America. De Gaulle had other ideas. While engaged with Germany in the construction of the European Community, he aspired to build a Euro-Arab strategic and economic bloc against America that would strengthen Europe with a tremendous power in international policy. General de Gaulle was motivated by the desire to maintain the centuries-old 'French Muslim' or 'Arab' policy that led in the 19th century to the building of a French Empire and to bloody rivalries with the British. After decolonisation in 1962, he was anxious to keep good relations with the former colonies as well as to protect French influence and markets throughout the Arab and Muslim world. In contact with Haj Amin, de Gaulle planned to detach the European Community from America in order to create a Euro-Arab common policy based on strategic and economic interests. In other words, the Arab-Mediterranean link would replace the Atlantic one.

The then seven countries of the EC were reluctant to follow French policy, which they judged anti-American and anti-Israeli. But in the 1970s French President Georges Pompidou, and later Valéry Giscard d'Estaing, succeeded along with Germany in bringing the nine countries of the EEC to accept this Euro-Arab rapprochement. Two events brought them to accept the French-Arab plan: a wave of Palestinian terrorism in European cities and the Arab oil boycott after the Yom Kippur War in October 1973. In November 1973, France and Germany issued a declaration in which they confirmed the European Community's readiness to open a dialogue with the Arab countries.[2] The Arab preconditions for opening such a dialogue and cancelling the oil boycott were that Europe should recognise Yassir Arafat as the sole representative of the Palestinians, support the PLO and Arab policy against Israel, and adopt a policy contrary to that of America as well as dissociate itself from the USA – a trend that de Gaulle had already championed since the late 1960s.

The development of an unofficial Euro-Arab strategy called the Euro-Arab Dialogue is recorded in documents published by the French Ministry of Foreign Affairs (*Documents de Politique Internationale*, Ministère des Affaires Etrangères, Paris) and in EC and EU documents.[3] The Dialogue brought forth numerous agreements in the economic, social, cultural and foreign policy sectors between the EC and the Arab League countries, as well as the development of Arab and Muslim immigration in the West. The EC hoped that the Euro-Arab symbiosis achieved through economic development, soft diplomacy and multiculturalism would guarantee peace, markets and oil.

The Euro-Arab Dialogue framework was enlarged in 1995 by the Mediterranean Partnership strategy, the so-called 'Barcelona Declaration', which was also signed by Israel. A network of associations and monitoring bodies linked to the European Commission and the Arab League were then created to implement the political and cultural fusion between Europe and the Arab countries. In this context Muslim immigration was welcomed in Europe as an element of a Mediterranean geo-strategy conducted as a partnership with the Arab-Muslim world on the basis of compromises, appeasement, and continual funding and services provided to the Palestinian and the Arab world, similar to the funds given to underdeveloped EU member-states. As a consequence, a massive Muslim immigration in Europe was correlated with a European strategy that professed that peace and stability in the Mediterranean depended on economic development in the Arab and Muslim world, political and financial support for the Palestinians, multiculturalism and multilateralism.

This policy of accommodation and moral relativism led to the grafting onto European societies of an Islamisation process that triggers the obliteration of European history and cultural identities. As stated before, such orientation was duplicated from the mechanisms that fostered European integration, in spite of the differences in culture and political ideologies between Europe and the Muslim South. In fact, it was the same ideological pattern, but applied in two different contexts: the European and the Muslim, as if the Muslim and Arab world were similar to that of the European states.

MULTICULTURALISM

Multiculturalism in the context of European integration is a positive process because it involves reciprocity between the different European cultures, which adopt the same deontology or historical instruments for self-criticism and adjust to the same values. Multiculturalism does not mean a suppression of history, but rather implies more historical and cultural objectivity.

However, multiculturalism of the Euro-Arab type superimposed onto the European integration process is not based on the principle of reciprocity, as that would imply a similar self-criticism of Muslim history and of relations with non-Muslim cultures and peoples. The duplication in a Muslim context of a policy that fostered European integration overlooks the difference in culture and political ideologies between Europe and the Arab and Muslim countries. Yet both dynamics – European integration and Euro-Arab Partnership – were conducted by the European Commission, which explains the ignorance by most Europeans of Europe's Arab and Muslim policy.

The concept of European integration implied the effacement of national and cultural identities in Europe itself – and this same concept presides over the creation of a new Euro-Arab civilisation, better known as 'Mediterranean Civilisation'. These two dynamics are similar, overlapping and intertwined processes, but in Europe multiculturalism functions at the intergovernmental level, while in the Euro-Arab symbiosis policy there is only a one-way process, since the Muslim countries increasingly proclaim their religious and nationalist characters, which of course impinge on their emigrants and prevent their integration.

Yet Europe continues to plan its new Mediterranean Civilisation where the identity will be 'Us'. Such process implies the destruction of a European social cohesion linked to Italian or British, French or German history and culture, in order to replace it by a de-nationalised Mediterranean entity sprung from multiculturalism and the death of history. Through immigration, Europe draws closer to the Muslim

South and East, while increasing its separation from America and losing its Judaeo-Christian spiritual roots and its secular freedoms. In order to impose on Europeans a multicultural Euro-Muslim civilisation – presumably to prevent war and the clash of civilisations that terrorises so much of Europe – the European Council has established a vast array of networks promoting dialogue, intertwining of populations at all levels, and multiculturalism. We notice that since the EU based its concept of peace and the increase of its supranational powers on destroying European nationalisms, it has also applied this same dynamic to the Euro-Arab context in order to create this Euro-Arab symbiosis.

On 19 June 2000, the European Council adopted a *Common Strategy on the Mediterranean Region* that reaffirmed this strategy of building peace by establishing a partnership in social, cultural and human affairs. The document states that 'particular attention will be paid to the media and universities' and requests that each incoming presidency of the European Council implement the Common Strategy with a view to reinforce the political, strategic and human links between the South (the Arab countries) and the North (Europe). One can notice here the drive to bring the media and the universities – i.e. culture – into line with politics.

The means to implement this cultural policy were stated in the *Report of 8 November 2002*, presented by the Spanish socialist, Luis Maria de Puig, to the European Parliamentary Assembly, where the trend to bring every domain of culture under the control and supervision of politics is clear. He petitioned for a new Euro-Arab writing of history, intensive exchanges of students and teachers, a Euro-Arab university and parliament, a strong symbiosis between intellectuals, a network of collaboration, actions and synergies between politicians, writers, artists, communicators, opinion leaders, NGOs and every sector of the arts (theatre, music, films), in order to glue together and bring about this new Euro-Arab Mediterranean civilisation. His report was accepted by the EU in January 2003, when the terrorist threat and the looming war in Iraq increased the urgency for dialogue.

The template of the new Mediterranean civilisation and the means to implement it in Europe were explained in a European Commission document of October 2003, *The Dialogue Between Peoples and Cultures in the Euro-Mediterranean Area,* which was accepted by the EU in December 2003. Written by 18 people, this text established the policy for the European continent and the future of half a billion people who have not even read it, but whose taxes are used to fund its policies. The authors promote common 'Euro-Arab values' and a shared culture based on a set of founding principles:

1. Respect for the Other.
2. Equality among states, peoples, cultures, individuals, between men and women, etc.
3. Total Freedom of conscience.
4. Solidarity of every kind and in every field.
5. Knowledge about the Other.

The writers call for an active support 'from heads of state to local associations and groups of citizens, parliamentary assemblies, trade-unions, non-governmental organisations' (p.22), to build the new society on these principles. According to the authors, the creation of this Euro-Arab Mediterranean civilisation requires the establishment of a **joint institutional system** (bold in the text, p.23) somehow similar to the EU institutions, as explained:

> There would be a Euro-Med Council for culture and education. [*It is paradoxical that, since the launch of Barcelona, only two sectoral ministerial conferences have been devoted to culture, while the ministers of education and research have never met BY.*]
>
> There would be a Euro-Med Parliamentary Assembly, with a powerful Committee on the dialogue between peoples and cultures.
>
> There would be a Foundation which, together with the Parliamentary Assembly, could draw the partners'

> attention to violations of the fundamental principles and, with the Council, draw up a programme of priorities, *and would have the task of independently assessing cultural programmes and the cultural impact of other measures (such as privatisation, opening up of trade, visa and immigration policy, and prevention of discrimination)*[emphasis by BY]. When performing its drafting role, the Foundation should take into account as much as possible the experiences and initiatives of local authorities, thus underlining the part they play, and will increasingly play, in the intercultural dialogue in everyday life.

The actors in civil society, organised along geographical or thematic lines, would have full access to each of these three joint institutions which, either separately or jointly, would have a much better perception of the difficulties and concerns of a true dialogue between peoples and cultures and the most effective ways to overcome them.[4]

The Anna Lindh Foundation[5] is the body that was created in December 2003 exactly for that purpose and along those lines. It will implement, under the supervision of the European Commission, the new Mediterranean society and culture, and will control its policies, culture, books, publications, teaching, universities and media. Hence the European populations will lose even more control over their culture, institutions, visa and immigration policy, which will be supervised by nebulous networks under the control of a vague Euro-Arab Mediterranean civilisation. And what do these 'fundamental principles' mean? Are Europeans requested to show solidarity with *shari'a* rules or with jihadist activities like those of Hezbollah or the Palestinian jihad that encompasses the jihad theological ideology, its strategy and tactics? Since history and culture represent the memory and soul of people it is important to examine whether there is a clash of two visions: the European view of history and the Islamic one.

A few months later, on 15 June 2004, the Austrian Secretary General of the Council of Europe, Walter

Schwimmer, declared to the ministers of the Organisation of the Islamic Conference (OIC) that the Islamic component is an integral part of Europe's diversity, and he asked them to consider joint projects on history teaching and religious diversity.

The triangular and interconnected poles of 'culture – immigration – policy' became pre-eminent after the murder of Theo van Gogh (October 2004) and the Cartoons affair (September 2005). In early December 2005 the OIC, which counts 56 Muslim countries plus the Palestinian Authority and represents over a billion Muslims, met in Mecca and issued several resolutions, amongst which were: 1) making the Palestinian problem a central issue; 2) building the unity and solidarity of the world *Umma* by rooting it in the Koran and the Sunna; 3) fighting Islamophobia at the international level; 4) asking the West to fight Islamophobia through the media and education.

On 7 February 2006, the OIC Observatory on Islamophobia issued a commentary entitled 'Freedom of Speech and Respect for Islamic Religion' (sic). It denounced 'the consistent pattern and continuity of sacrilege and blasphemy being committed in the name of freedom of speech by some publications in Europe'. It requests the immediate halt to such acts by asking the leaders of the countries concerned to condemn them:

> From the perspective of 1.3 billion Muslims, blasphemy is outside the domain of decency and freedom of speech. It may also be noted that it is not the religious dogma which Muslims are protecting but it is part of their core belief to maintain respect for their Prophet at any cost. The blasphemy attacks the heart of Islamic Humanism and its founder Muhammad (PBUH)[6] whose teaching was foremost among the world teachers as divine messenger of God.

Hence the clash of cultures, if not of religions, has become a prominent issue between secular Europeans and Muslim on one hand and traditional Muslim immigrants. Already in

August 2005, Doudou Diène of Senegal, UN Special Rapporteur of the Commission on Human Rights on racism, xenophobia and related intolerance, had submitted a report to the UN General Assembly where he drew attention to two developments of particular concern: the rise in racism and xenophobia as a result of identity constructs; and the mistreatments of aliens, asylum-seekers, refugees and immigrants. He attributed the rise of racism to the identity factor and called the attention of 'European Union member States to the urgency of giving special attention, in building the identity of the new Europe, to its ethnic, cultural and religious pluralism'. He highlighted the danger of racism 'under the guise of combating terrorism, defending the "national identity", promoting "national preference" and combating illegal immigration'. He condemned the impact of xenophobic trends in 'legislation and administrative and security practices that criminalise non-nationals, immigrants, refugees and asylum-seekers'.

Such accusations were emphasised in his UN report to the General Assembly on 20 September 2006, in which he denounced religious defamation and the impact of the fight against terrorism on human rights. He judges negative 'the trend and sometimes the ideological position of many Governments to consider that the security of the country and its people constitute the sum and substance of all human rights. Thus, all human rights guaranteed by international instruments are interpreted and implemented in the light of their relevance and contribution to the fight against terrorism.'

For Doudou Diène, the basic foundation governing the 'living together' of all societies is the respect of the rights of others. He criticises the new security context that undermines the respect of human rights, and deplores the discrimination practised over two main issues: security and identity. His report does not mention the fact that terrorism, the right to kill indiscriminately, is the greatest violation of human rights and that illegal immigration is also a violation of the laws of a national group. For Diène, the defence of national identity, the fight against terrorism and illegal immigration obstruct the general trend towards multiculturalism.

EU leaders could not have been more receptive to such criticism. They think that increasing dialogues at all levels, developing multiculturalism and immigration, as well as the mixing of populations and the dilution of national identities, will guarantee world peace. The fanatical outburst provoked by the satirical cartoons prompted Javier Solana to have a long conversation with Mr Ihsanoglu, the OIC's secretary general, on 2 February 2006, when both agreed to cooperate against Islamophobia. In spite of this promise, the wave of violence started the next day worldwide, with killings (at least 50 people died) and destruction as a demonstration of power to the West.

With the increased clout of terrorism in 2006, the EU maintained stolidly its Mediterranean political orientation and enlarged its split from the United States, while fomenting an anti-Israeli vilification campaign through its funded NGOs' countless networks.[7] Following the recommendations of the OIC, the EU prepared in April a lexicon for public communication where terms like 'jihad' and 'Islamic terrorism' were banned. The lexicon provides guidelines to EU officials in order to prevent offending Muslims.

At an EU conference in Berlin in November 2006, to plan the *European Year of Intercultural Dialogue* scheduled for 2008, the participants examined the opportunities to define and intensify the European Union's cultural content. The conference agreed that a common foreign policy and development policy should be based on Europe's cultural values. Richard von Weizsäcker, former president of Germany (1984–94), declared that Europe should be able to prevent the clash of civilisations by replacing it with dialogue. The political potential of culture would be the basis of its foreign policy. The conference concluded that cultural action would be a basic element of foreign and development policy.[8] At the conference it was pointed out 'that immigrants could have a stronger allegiance to Europe and its values than to the particular Member State in which they settle, a concept that has clear implications for the development of citizenship'. Would therefore the de-nationalised and religiously rootless European values be a condition for immigrants' integration and a prerequisite for foreign policy?

For this reason, the themes chosen for the year 2008 were racism, xenophobia, asylum, immigration – and multiculturalism, of course. A multiplicity of programmes on intercultural dialogue in numerous sectors was planned to contribute to innovation in every dimension. The conference ruled that 'Mechanisms will be set in place to monitor and report on the progress of the European institutions and Member States in implementing concrete initiatives and in investing significantly in the European cultural space.'

The planning of the European Year of Intercultural Dialogue (2008) was decided by the European Parliament and the Council of the European Union, and published in the *Official Journal of the European Union* on 30 December 2006. It states that 'Intercultural dialogue thus contributes towards achieving a number of the EU strategic priorities, in particular by: respecting and promoting cultural diversity in Europe, improving coexistence and encouraging active European citizenship open to the world and based on the common values in the EU' (§5). It also enables 'the EU to make its voice better heard in the world and to forge effective partnerships with countries in its neighbourhood', a policy that is seen as extending a zone of stability and common prosperity beyond the EU.

Among many other goals, the dialogue would combat exclusion, racism and xenophobia, and would set policy on asylum and help the integration of immigrants as well as human rights (§6). Point 9 states that 'the notion of "active European citizenship" should cover not only citizens of the EU as defined in Article 17 of the EC Treaty, but any individual living permanently or temporarily in the EU'. Among the many objectives listed are the development of an active European citizenship open to the world, respect for cultural diversity and the highlighting of the contribution of different cultures. Ten million euros were budgeted for these activities.

The Anna Lindh Foundation (ALF) is the flagship for the Euro-Arab dialogue strategy. Its Executive Director, Dr

Traugott Schoefthaler, presented some proposals after consultation with the national ALF networks, regional partners, the Advisory Committee and a high-level expert group convened along with the Arab League. He pointed to the misconception of 'Europe versus Islam', 'as if Europe's identity would not also have Islamic roots and present features', and the need to de-legitimise 'any association of cultures and religions with terrorism' – a point strongly argued by the OCI and the Alliance of Civilisations. Schoefthaler indicated that already the ALF counts 35 national networks bringing together 1200 institutions and organisations bent on dialogue. It has established, together with the Council of Europe and the Arab League Educational, Cultural and Scientific Organisation (ALECSO), a EuroMed teacher training programme on cultural and religious diversity, from which 400 teachers from 35 countries have benefited.[9]

This position echoes the requests of Doudou Diène and of the OCI regarding the multicultural identity of Europe and its duty to fight Islamophobia. The frenzy of dialogues and soul-searching on Europe's multicultural identity, with its Islamic component, appears to culminate in the compliance of the EU to the demands of the OCI. The aim is a vast campaign of re-education of the Europeans. Yet, none of these efforts toward multiculturalism are planned in the 56 countries of the OCI, which are building the unity and solidarity of the world *Umma* on the Koran and the Sunna.

To these activities must be added the endeavours of the newly-formed Alliance of Civilisations created to oppose the clash of civilisations, on the initiative of José Luis Rodriguez Zapatero, immediately after the Madrid jihadist bombing in March 2004. On 13 November 2006, the High-Level Group of the Alliance of Civilisations presented a report pointing to a context prevalent between Western and Muslim societies, making people feel persistent discrimination, humiliation or marginalisation. The 'root causes' include the Israeli-Palestinian conflict, 'which remains one of the gravest threats to international stability'. Western military operations in Muslim countries, and the perception of double standards in the application of international law, have increased the resentment among Muslims. The report also mentions specific societal, religious and political issues in the Muslim world, and formulates recommendations that again echo the OIC requests. Foremost, the international community is urgently invited to settle the Israeli-Palestinian conflict using the mechanisms proposed by the Report. Inflammatory language that feeds tensions between Muslim and Western societies should be avoided. Programmes for training journalists in intercultural understanding should be created, balanced coverage encouraged. Media and education should conform to guidelines for fairness. Neither materials that denigrate other faiths, nor those accounts of the historical past that ignore the contribution of other cultures and nations, should remain unchallenged. To combat discrimination, media campaigns should be developed: 'The High-Level Group urges American and European universities to expand research into the significant contributions of immigrant communities to American and European life. Such research should support media campaigns highlighting the social, cultural and economic contributions of immigrants and the benefits of cultural diversity.'[10]

The longer version of the report stresses that 'During medieval times, Islamic civilisation was a major source of innovation, knowledge acquisition, and scientific advancement that contributed to the emergence of the Renaissance and the Enlightenment in Europe.' Peaceful co-existence was the hallmark of relations between Christianity, Islam and Judaism from their earliest period until today. Under Muslim rule, Christians and Jews were largely free to practise their faiths. The report condemns strongly selective accounts that putatively paint mutually exclusive faith communities: 'Such distorted historical narratives must be countered', because 'this history does not offer explanations for current conflicts or for the rise in hostility between Western and Muslim societies. On the contrary, the roots of these phenomena lie in the developments that took place in the 19th and 20th centuries, beginning with European imperialism, the resulting emergence of anti-colonial movements, and the legacy of the confrontations between them' (p.11). Strangely, all the tremendous onslaughts committed by jihad on three continents and throughout the centuries vanish from human consciousness. Incriminations continue with the establishment of Israel, the 'occupation', and disproportionate retaliation against human bombs. Most of the recommendations seem to be addressed to the EU and concern the need to reform education, welcome migrants and develop multiculturalism and the responsibility of the media.

Yet Europe has been under jihadist attacks since the eighth century. If we deny this, we deny more than a millennium of European history. The orthodox Muslim view on jihad was reaffirmed at the UN in Geneva on 21 September 2006 by Ambassador Masood Khan of Pakistan, speaking on behalf of the OIC at the second session of the new Human Rights Council on 'Incitement to racial and religious hatred and the promotion of tolerance'. He stressed: '1) Islam was not spread by the sword; 2) that Islam forbids violence in all its forms; 3) that jihad is an individual's quest for spiritual reform or the right to self-defence.'

Reading all these reports, one senses a tremendous pressure on the Europeans, constantly infiltrating the schools and universities, the media and public opinion, through well-organised networks. Professors are expelled if they diverge from the guidelines, journalists feel tracked, writers are boycotted, bookshops refuse to sell some books, lawyers and judges are confused by multiculturalist rule according to *shari'a* law – as happened in Munich.[11] Censorship, insecurity and fear are everywhere. In schools, teachers stop teaching the Holocaust, the Armenian genocide and the Crusades, and have to adapt to Muslim customs in the name of multiculturalism.

The vigorous and healthy unending debate on history is suppressed and replaced by an imposed Muslim interpretation of Western history that eliminates 13 centuries of countless Jewish, Christian, Hindu, Arab and Turkish documents carefully studied, commented on, classified and conserved in Western libraries. Are we going to destroy them because they contradict Muslim historical theses? Will the whole culture and memory of Europe be thrown out in order to adopt the Muslim one? Are we going back to the time of the *auto da fé*? Already witch-hunts threaten those who fight for freedom of opinion.

Yet multiculturalism is not practised in Muslim countries. Millions of European non-Muslim migrants there would not be welcome and the recent decisions of the OCI to build the unity of the world *Umma* on the Koran and the Sunna is totally opposed to what they are demanding from the West. Can peace be built by imposing multiculturalism on one partner and not on the other? Will the *madrassas* start to teach Voltaire and Spinoza? What sort of multiculturalism exists in Saudi Arabia, Iran, Pakistan, Egypt? And in our multicultural societies, are we going to refer to two types of human rights: one inspired by the *shari'a* and the other based on secular laws?

A consequence of this policy is the denial of the Islamic jihad and of its dangers; this denial is fundamental to Eurabian policy. The reason is that the EC was created to eliminate inter-European war. But this same European consensus for peace was transferred to another context, represented by European relations with its Arab neighbours. However, Muslim societies do not share the European consensus for peace that emerged after the two world wars. The Eurabian refusal to face the jihadist threat motivated an appeasement policy and a peaceful surrender to jihadists, while pretending that Europe's enemies were American, but above all Israeli, policies.

Moreover, European leaders claim that Islam is part of Europe. This assertion is necessary to the Euro-Arab symbiosis of the Mediterranean project that – according to Eurabian belief – guarantees peace. They think peace is a matter of continual European concessions on its culture and identities, and of its own disintegration. Yet how European identity is defined is very important, because if it includes Islam it will legitimise the development of mosques, *madrassas* and a *shari'a* parallel culture and policy in Europe. In other words, is Islam returning rightfully to its European homeland, or rather does it represent a foreign immigrant population that ought to integrate into the majority indigenous population?

In an essay, 'A Battle for Global Values', British Prime Minister Tony Blair found it incredible that much Western opinion professes that the emergence of global terrorism is somehow the fault of the West, or of Israel, or caused by poverty.[12] This is, in fact, exactly what the Report of the Alliance of Civilisations affirms. Blair lamented a Western opinion blinded by Islamist propaganda – as if this situation did not result from 30 years of deliberate European policy of dialogue, concessions and compromises within the Euro-Arab alliances. How can one criticise jihad if one is allied to and supports the countries that promote it?

On the BBC, on 7 January 2007, Gordon Brown said he believed the ideological battle for the hearts and minds of young Muslims was as crucial as the battle against Communism in previous generations.[13] But he forgets that the ideological war against Communism implied a harsh attack on Communist ideology and policies. How can this be done with Islamism without being accused of Islamophobia or even worse, without transgressing the Islamic blasphemy law applied unofficially in Europe, or without provoking a terrorist revenge?

Susan Emanuel edited this chapter

CHAPTER 7

'TAUGHT BY NO PROFESSORS AND ILLUSTRATED BY NO EXAMPLES': THE BRITISH ABOLITION OF SLAVERY

CANON PETER WILLIAMS

The 18th-century triangular slave trade was immense in scale and profitability so far as Britain was concerned. Goods were shipped from Europe to Africa and exchanged for slaves; slaves were taken to the West Indies; tobacco and sugar were brought back to Europe. By the mid-18th century, Bristol and Liverpool had outstripped London by becoming the leading slave trading centres in Europe. This produced vast wealth and an immense hinterland of connected businesses in tobacco, sugar, cotton, ship-building, insurance and finance to service the industry directly, and pottery, guns, brass and silk to provide the goods to be exported. Bristol grew three-fold throughout the 18th century and a major factor was the slave trade and its allied industries. But it was Liverpool that emerged as the slave centre. As the 18th century progressed, its physical advantages as a port led to its becoming equal to that of Bristol and London combined, taking some 60 per cent of the British trade and 40 per cent of the European trade. In the ten years from 1783 its proceeds from the African trade topped £12 million, from 873 voyages and the sale of 300,000 Africans.

Eric Williams judged that the profits from the triangular trade 'fertilised the entire productive system of the country'.[1] While more recent work has established that the commercial risks were not inconsiderable, that profits were seldom in the bonanza category and that the role of the slave trade in financing the Industrial Revolution was much less substantial than was once thought, nonetheless it was, with its returns of between 8 and 10 per cent, a very profitable industry. It was furthermore widely regarded as being extremely important to the economic well-being of the country and was umbilically connected to an area that was enormously valuable to the imperial economy – namely the West Indies. By 1770, Niall Ferguson judges, 'Britain's Atlantic empire seemed to have found a natural equilibrium. The triangular trade between Britain, West Africa and the Caribbean kept the plantations supplied with labour. The mainland American colonies kept them supplied with victuals. Sugar and tobacco streamed back to Britain, a substantial proportion for re-export to the Continent. And the profits from these New World commodities oiled the wheels of the Empire's Asian commerce.'[2] Ferguson roundly rejects the thesis, beloved of those who prefer to see history as a matter of impersonal economic forces rather than a product of human decisions and determination, that the slave trade was abolished because it was unprofitable. All the evidence, he maintains, 'points the other way: in fact, it was abolished despite the fact that it was still profitable'.[3]

That a nation should be brought to a place where it acted so decisively against the dictates of its long-established historic and current economic self-interest is something quite amazing. Of course there were many factors that brought about this profound change in the ethics of a people, and these we will seek to examine in what follows. But by far the single and most decisive reason for the change was that the campaign to abolish first the slave trade and then slavery itself was driven by a number of people who were endowed with remarkable and very varied capacities, who shared common ideological passions – among which the cause of abolition was but one – who were driven by an over-arching evangelical theology which most of them shared, and who were linked together by common friendships of great depth. This, in the words of Roger Anstey, impelled them 'to act in the cause of abolition with a zeal and a perseverance which other men could rarely match'.[4]

There is no doubt that by the time the anti-slavery movement began to gather momentum in the last decades of the

18th century the case for slavery appeared much less convincing than it once had. Indeed, in a remarkable change from 100 years earlier, there was virtually no significant moral justification of slavery – even by its defenders. The defence, still immensely strong, had become pragmatic rather than moral. Slavery had existed from time immemorial and was a part of the imperfect human condition. The change was a consequence partly of Enlightenment convictions about liberty. As, in the words of Montesquieu, 'all men are born equal', slavery must be unnatural.[5] And this was echoed by eminent English thinkers such as the jurist William Blackstone, the philosopher William Paley and the political philosopher Edmund Burke. Furthermore, Adam Smith, the moral philosopher, gave such thinking an economic direction in his argument that, despite appearances to the contrary, slavery was the dearest form of labour because a 'person who can acquire no property, can have no other interest but to eat as much, and to labour as little as possible'.[6] Add in the utilitarian concern with happiness and benevolence and there was an intellectual climate which could find no justification for slavery.

Many Christians shared these Enlightenment convictions. And this certainly included the evangelicals who became so prominent in the abolitionist movement. In particular, as David Bebbington has convincingly argued, they echoed its broadly optimistic view of the world, believing 'that humanity enjoyed great potential for improvement'[7] and that benevolence, happiness and liberty were primary human objectives.[8]

Though evangelicals accepted these current cultural ideas, it is important to emphasise that they did so because they believed them to have a deep theological provenance. That for them meant being writ large on the pages of Scripture. If there was an overlap with current culture, the evangelicals had also many convictions that were not shared within the accepted wisdom of their day. It is necessary now to seek to discern these. Their distinctive convictions hinged around two areas.

First, there was their understanding of sin, redemption, salvation and the consequential commitment to God. A starting place for evangelicals was an awareness of their sinfulness, followed by a personal faith in the redemption that the Lord Jesus Christ has purchased, followed by a commitment to live a life of love and obedience. Within this the exodus story of the delivery of the people of Israel from bondage in Egypt was critical. In that deliverance from slavery God's gracious love was decisive. In response the Israelites were commanded to love those who were experiencing bondage and captivity. And what was true for them must be true for those who followed the Lord's teaching in the 18th century. They were even more called to be benevolent and to work for the happiness of their fellow creatures because they had a greater revelation of God's love in Christ. The New Testament was an even more profound story of benevolent love leading to deliverance from the slavery of sin and Satan, and the redemption of salvation through Christ the Saviour. This of course was freedom from the shackles of spiritual slavery, but that made evangelicals particularly sensitive to the issues of physical slavery.

This identification with physical slavery was for the evangelical, argues Anstey, 'a necessary externalisation of the polar opposites of his own religious experience at its deepest level'.[9] While this is something of an over-statement, for clearly it was not a necessary externalisation for all,[10] the enormous power of the biblical account of redemption and of deliverance from slavery in the intellectual climate of the late 18th century cannot be gainsaid. And the proof lies in the frequency with which the evangelicals used the imagery and metaphors that gather round it to press home their anti-slavery cause.

Much was made too of the fact that all are made in the image of God. 'Am I not a man and a brother?' asked the negro kneeling in chains in the famous Wedgwood cameo of the time. And from that was but a step to an emphasis on the need for liberty for all. 'Liberty', trumpeted John Wesley, 'is the right of every human creature, as soon as he breathes the vital air; and no human law can deprive him of that right which he derives from the law of nature'.[11] There was then no truck with the idea of African inferiority. Evangelicals, in brief, had come to Enlightenment conclusions about liberty, benevolence and happiness, but by a different route. Consequently, as Davis puts it, 'early anti-slavery writers like James Ramsay and Granville Sharp repeatedly identified the theory of racial inferiority with Hume, Voltaire, and materialistic philosophy in general; they explicitly presented their attacks on slavery as a vindication of Christianity, moral accountability, and the unity of mankind'.[12] They took, in brief, Enlightenment values, gave them a different base and, in Anstey's words, transposed and supercharged them[13] in a way which made them a 'formidable force' when they 'turned to political action against the slave trade'.[14]

The second area was the evangelical belief in Providence, and the sense of obligation, responsibility, duty and judgement that they were placed under as individuals and that their country was placed under as a nation. By Providence, evangelicals referred to their conviction that God was actively involved in the world. As well as God's superintendence of the world, or his general providence, there was his particular providence – his ordering of the world so that it manifested his mercy, or his challenge to embark on a certain pathway, or his judgement.

Thus Wilberforce was acutely aware of 'accidents' and 'contingencies' as he looked back on his life, and of the fact, for example, that had his religious change come a year earlier then he would not have become a Member of Parliament, 'nor should I have adopted the methods by which I ingratiated myself in the good will of some of my chief supporters'.[15]

This sense of God going before and giving opportunities to make the right choices gave a huge sense of purpose and security to those who believed it. It presented an equally enormous challenge because it was so easily possible to choose one's own selfish way rather than to seek the Lord's way. What was true for individuals was true also of nations. There would be judgement for sinful actions. The title of one of Granville Sharp's books makes this point with chilling directness: *The Law of Retribution: A Serious Warning to Great Britain and her Colonies, founded on unquestionable examples of God's Temporal Vengeance against Tyrants,*

Slaveholders and Oppressors (1776). James Stephen, to take a later example, warmed to the theme of adverse national consequences resulting from decisions which caused 'the displeasure of Heaven'. England, he reflected, had experienced the French Revolution and the 'fatal wars that have ensued', had known the subversion of 'the prosperity, the peace, and the security', had endured 'singular evils' '*ever since our first refusal to abolish the slave trade*', and was at the moment of writing threatened by 'still greater evils'.[16]

These evangelicals, then, had a deep experience of Christ's redemption from the slavery of sin in their lives, an enormous sense that their privileges carried with them responsibilities to work for the release of those who were in both spiritual and physical slavery, and a total commitment to discovering the Lord's purpose for them. These were combined with an impregnable trust in his providential care for them as they pursued that purpose. It was these qualities which gave them such a central role in a movement that was both at the same time bigger than them and could not be explained without them.

We now need to place them in a more precise historical and intellectual context, for it was that context which enabled them to interpret their theological convictions in a way they had scarcely considered before.

It is necessary to remind ourselves that the abolitionist movement was a product of the late 18th and early 19th centuries. Prior to that, neither Christianity nor evangelicalism, as one of its substrata, had been at all predisposed to regard slavery as necessarily against God's will. Thus John Newton is often thought of as being part of the abolitionist cause, and he was, but only late in his career and after he had written 'Amazing Grace'. George Whitefield kept slaves.[17] A catalyst was needed to raise moral awareness of the evils of slavery. That catalyst was, as is well known, American Quakers. Increasingly they began to condemn slavery and to argue the case most cogently. One of their number, Anthony Benezet, was particularly effective, with his *Historical Account of Guinea* (1771) giving a vivid account of slavery and its 'lamentable effects'. Bolstered by his *A Caution to Great Britain*, it had a profound theological resonance, as attention was drawn to the guilt against providence which 'lies upon our nation generally' and upon individuals who in any degree 'countenance this aggravated iniquity'.[18] Benezet was a major influence in stirring John Wesley to write his *Thoughts Upon Slavery* in 1774. Wesley used all his passionate rhetorical skills to denounce slavery and to drive home the point that slavery was an offence against a just God, an offence which would bring retribution from that just God, who 'will reward every man according to his works'.[19] John Wesley of course was very influential and, to take one example, may have been a key factor in Newton's conversion to the anti-slavery cause.[20]

And these ripples of influence widened. In 1785, Thomas Clarkson, a young Cambridge graduate, was writing a prize essay with the title, 'Is it right to make slaves of others against their will?' The fact that this title was set well illustrates the intellectual discomfort with slavery which we have already noted. The fact that Clarkson soon discovered Benezet as a major source, and that the impact on him was to turn 'a trial of academical reputation' into a work 'which might be useful to injured Africa',[21] demonstrates the interaction of Enlightenment questioning with a growing conviction among evangelicals that something had to be done. Clarkson was haunted by what his genius for painstaking investigation had revealed about the horrors of slavery. 'Then surely some person should interfere', he kept repeating, as he increasingly felt that he was that person.[22] He made contact with anti-slavery Quakers who introduced him to Granville Sharp.

Sharp was arguably the first figure to move an intellectual and theological debate and polemic into a coherent and practical cause. He had himself experienced both Quaker and evangelical influences. He was, in Reddie's apt description, a 'quirky' individual.[23] He was adversarial and courageous. He was emotional and erratic, with a somewhat unbalanced interest in Old Testament prophecies. He was also patient, persistent and personable. And, though he was not a lawyer, he had a highly developed legal cast of mind. In 1772 he took up the case of John Somerset, a slave who ran away in London and was then recaptured by his master. The question of legal moment was whether a master had the right forcibly to remove a slave from England. Sharp took on the case and won in spectacular fashion, with Lord Mansfield giving his famous judgment: 'No master ever was allowed here to take a slave by force to be sold abroad because he deserted from his service ... and therefore the man must be discharged,' with its ringing conclusion, 'Let justice be done, though the Heavens may fall.' As importantly, Sharp had a direction for his talents as he got the slavery issue raised in the House of Commons, petitioned bishops and took up cases which were likely to further the anti-slavery cause in the courts.

The combination of a substantial group of Quakers committed to the anti-slavery movement, with energetic, persistent and well-informed individuals such as Clarkson and Sharp, led naturally enough to the setting up of the Abolition Committee in May 1787. Immediately it focused on the abolition of the slave trade (as opposed to slavery) and the rousing of people to the anti-slavery cause – 'especially', it noted, 'those from whom any alteration must proceed – the Members of our Legislature'.[24] And here they were weak, both because they had no parliamentarians among their number and because Parliament, as Wesley had realistically judged just a few years earlier, had so many causes 'which seem of greater importance ... that they are not likely to attend to this'.[25] But Clarkson had already begun to persuade William Wilberforce of the strength of the abolitionist case.

Born into a wealthy mercantile family in Hull, Wilberforce enjoyed a privileged education where – despite his diminutive 5ft 2in stature – his high intelligence, easy charm, beautiful voice, brilliant wit, sharp mimicry skills and outstanding conversational and inter-personal gifts made him a popular and leading figure among the movers and shakers of his generation. It so happened these particular movers and shakers were extremely talented, and some advanced, seemingly effortlessly, to the highest prominence in the shortest period of time in the whole of British democratic history.

William Pitt the Younger, to take the most outstanding example, became prime minister in 1783 at the age of 24. He was one of Wilberforce's closest friends. It was a natural step for Wilberforce to enter Parliament in 1780 as member for Hull at the age of 21. Much later Pitt judged that Wilberforce had 'the greatest natural eloquence' of anyone that he had ever known,[26] and that eloquence, quickly apparent, together with his very close friendship with Pitt, marked him out as someone eminently capable and extremely likely to reach the highest office.

His life was a mixture of slightly indolent ease and much socialising, with occasional glimpses of high moral and political purpose, and an increasingly sceptical religious mind-set. And then came, in Wilberforce's own language, the 'singular accident' and the 'contingencies'[27] which over an 18-month period brought together people and events which caused Wilberforce totally to review his life. It was a slow and painful religious process. He seemed, in his own self-description, 'to have awakened ... from a dream, to have recovered, as it were, the use of' his 'reason after a delirium', to have shaken off the desire for fame and distinction, to realise that he was 'an accountable being', that he would 'hereafter' have 'to appear at the bar of God', and that it was incumbent on him to examine the claims of Christianity.[28] He read widely, finding Bishop Butler and Pascal especially helpful, talked deeply with his intellectual guide, Isaac Milner, and then with his spiritual mentor, John Newton. He came to a settled mind slowly. But by Good Friday 1786 he was sufficiently committed to take communion.

His conversion, for that is what it was, had classic evangelical characteristics and consequences. He was soon recommending that the Bible should be 'the criterion of our opinions and actions'.[29] His faith was centred on the Saviour 'who died upon the Cross to atone for our transgressions'. And he sought by 'prayer and self-abasement' to allow this reality 'to soften, to animate, to warm my dull heart'.[30] It was now his 'constant prayer' that God would 'enable me to serve him more steadily, and my fellow-creatures more assiduously'.[31] The word 'duty' began to be heard frequently on his lips. But discerning where his duty lay was far from easy as his new evangelical friends gave him contradictory advice. The majority advised him to give up his old life with all the temptations that Parliament and public affairs would necessarily bring. Thus he contemplated ordination. John Newton, however, with extraordinary perspicacity, urged him 'to avoid at present making many religious acquaintances, widely separat[ing] from old friends ... [to] keep up [your] connection with Pitt, and to continue in Parliament'.[32] Wilberforce battled the issue through in prayer, in Bible reading and in conversation with friends, very much including the Prime Minister, Pitt. 'Surely', Pitt shrewdly, tellingly and persuasively observed, 'the principles as well as the practice of Christianity are simple, and lead not to meditation only but to action'.[33]

Wilberforce had had a concern about slavery going back to his early teenage years and this had been given a moral fillip by reading some of the contemporary accounts that were printed in the 1780s. Pitt, who was becoming increasingly persuaded of the anti-slavery cause, suggested to Wilberforce that he should take up the cause, and about that time Wilberforce became convinced that 'God Almighty' had set before him 'two great objects, the suppression of the slave trade and the reformation of manners'.[34] Historians debate what factor was most crucial in this determination, but the whole logic of Wilberforce's movement from political dilettante concerned with self-advancement to moral crusader concerned to fulfil a God-given destiny surely supports the judgement of his biographer sons that it came about as 'the immediate consequences of his altered character'.[35]

It was to be a long struggle – 20 years to the abolition of the British slave trade, and another 26 before full abolition of slavery was achieved. It is way beyond the scope of this chapter to do more than draw out a few over-arching points from the abolitionist struggle.

First, it was a very difficult struggle because, though the intellectual battle had been won, the pragmatic and self-interest battle certainly had not. The enormous damage that the abolition of the slave trade would inflict on the British economy and the British way of life was a point frequently reiterated. Something a good deal more dynamic and persistent than intellectual conviction by itself was required. The cause was made all the more difficult because of the retreat in the 1790s, even of its key back-room supporter, Pitt, to a much more cautious and conservative position in the light of the French Revolution and the subsequent wars. Wilberforce showed magnanimity of mind in granting that for Pitt 'other interests occupied more his thoughts and feelings ... I can truly however declare that he ... never produced in my mind any suspicion of lukewarmness in his opinion or feeling on the question.'[36]

Second, it was a very difficult struggle because there was no precedent to provide methodological templates. In the late 1830s Sir James Stephen put the reality facing the pioneers in elegant prose: 'in later days, agitation for the accomplishment of great political objects has taken a place among social arts. But sixty years since, it was among the inventions slumbering in the womb of time, taught by no professors, and illustrated by no examples.'[37] The genius of the pioneers was to discover a whole raft of new methods which have remained part of the weaponry of single-issue campaigners down to our own day. There were monster meetings and monster petitions. There were slogans and logos. There was formidable research. There were reports, articles, poems – and indeed the use of every medium that was currently available. There was networking and lobbying on a vast scale. Indeed, it is not an exaggeration to say that they invented, laid the foundations and built the superstructure of modern lobbying.

There was, linking with this, a willingness to form alliances with all sorts of unlikely people. There were *ad hominem* arguments about the advantages to England of dispensing with the slave trade which were not believed by many then and which distinguished historians today equally discount. They thus, in Anstey's telling description, concealed altruism 'beneath the cloak of interest'.[38] There was enormous creative energy, driven, yes, by huge commitment to a cause, but in the end only explicable by a rock-like confidence that this was God's calling. So the many disappointments, failures and frustrations were not allowed to become fatal blows, but were used rather as opportunities to rethink, regroup, restrategise and remotivate. As his opponent Stephen Fuller shrewdly observed of Wilberforce, defeat was not accepted as the final word because he possessed 'a very sufficient quantity of that enthusiastic spirit which is so far from yielding, that it grows more vigorous from blows'.[39]

Third, they had a rich galaxy of complementary skills. There were the indefatigable investigators like Clarkson. There were persuasive writers like Stephens and Macaulay. There were rich financiers like Henry Thornton. There were the inspired publicists like Josiah Wedgwood. There were influential pastor/theologians like John Newton. There were skilled parliamentarians like William Wilberforce. The inner core was the so-called Clapham Sect. Its members lived in the same area, shared close evangelical beliefs and were often inter-related.

Wilberforce was the central figure within this galaxy. Though he was much vilified by his opponents, he was ever-prepared to bring together, as he put it, 'all men who are like-minded, and who may probably at some time or other combine and concert for the public good',[40] and he was thus able to make common cause with philosophical opposites. Sometimes he was inclined, in consequence, to make compromises which greatly exasperated his more rigorous colleagues, though they accepted his judgement. One of his many gifts was to write and speak in a way which retained a respect and understanding for his opponents. Thus he wrote a particularly effective appeal in 1823 where he, in the words of Belmonte, 'winsomely infused his pamphlet with kindness and forbearance toward those he hoped to persuade that the institution of slavery was a great moral evil. He condemned the institution without appearing to condemn those who owned slaves.'[41]

Fourth, a particular skill of this group was to juxtapose the evidence about contemporary slavery with the arguments which came from their own Christian convictions and which resonated with their followers. They succeeded, as Coffey puts it, 'because they produced compelling evidence of the cruelty of the trade' and 'relayed' this 'to a wide audience in harrowing narratives of human suffering'.[42] That is not, however, a reason to accept Hochschild's argument that in so doing a case based on human empathy replaced a case based on their understanding of the biblical texts.[43] What they did rather was to join an appeal to human empathy with the biblical texts in a way which was totally congruous with those texts. If, Coffey asks with compelling logic, religious argument did not stir people in itself, 'why did abolitionists give it so much space? For', he continues, 'in publication after publication, critics of the slave trade quoted Scripture and rooted their campaign in Christian values and ideals'.[44]

Fifth, this was a moral crusade. It was not a crusade for political advantage, nor for economic prosperity, nor for greater world-power. Indeed, the likelihood was that any of these would be diminished as the cause was achieved. Wilberforce succeeded most brilliantly in presenting this moral case in a speech in the House of Commons in 1789:

> Policy, however ... is not my principle, and I am not ashamed to say it. There is a principle above every thing that is political ... [When] I reflect on the command which says, "Thou shalt do no murder," believing the authority to be divine, how can I dare to set up any reasonings of my own against it? And ... when we think of eternity, and of the future consequences of all human conduct, what is there in this life that should make any man contradict the dictates of his conscience, the principles of justice, the laws of religion, and of God ...
>
> [T]he nature and all the circumstances of this trade are now laid open to us; we can no longer plead ignorance – we cannot evade it – it is now an object placed before us – we cannot pass it; we may spurn it, we may kick it out of the way, but we cannot turn aside so as to avoid seeing it ... [It] is brought now so directly before our eyes, that this House must decide, and must justify to all

the world, and to their own consciences, the rectitude of the grounds and principles of their decision.

Burke commented that the speech 'equalled anything he had heard in modern times, and was not, perhaps, to be surpassed in the remains of Grecian eloquence'.[45] And the House was deeply impressed.

Such speeches and such organisation did not, as we now know, bring slavery rapidly to an end. Its full abolition was still 44 years away. There were to be many 'downs'. The anti-abolitionist cause made much more sense in the light of the pressures of the French threat. There were too many 'ups'. But there was a significant move forward in the opening decade of the 19th century, as the abolitionist cause gained a firm foothold in the psyche of the English people. This was a product of many things. The old-fashioned slave trade sat most uneasily with the new methods and approach of the Industrial Revolution. The argument that slavery was actually economically *disadvantageous* now seemed more compelling to many. Perhaps that was in part because the case that it was *morally* indefensible – and therefore highly damaging to the well-being of the nation – had also become measurably more popular. This new idealism was itself a product of the growing influence of the evangelical religious revival in all sections of society. Politically, the death of William Pitt and his replacement by Lord Grenville meant that there was now a prime minister disinclined to accept the case that the cause of abolition could be endlessly protracted. And that combination of factors brought the decision to end the slave trade with effect from 1 May 1807.

That of course did not bring the end of slavery. It did, however, bring to an end the first phase of the campaign. It was a considerable time before the second phase effectively began. This was because many, including Wilberforce, believed that the end of the slave trade marked the beginning of the end of slavery itself. It took time for that belief to be tested and found wanting. There was anti-slavery fatigue. There were other pressing causes which competed for the attention of 'the saints in politics', as they were often called. The political and international climates were not propitious to another move forward. A great deal of British energy was very properly given to patrolling the West African coast and seeking to persuade other nations to join Britain in its anti-slave trade commitment. There were some, most notably Thomas Clarkson, who never abandoned their belief that slavery as such needed to be abolished. By 1823 the evidence that this was true had begun to be overwhelming.

Wilberforce was persuaded. He wrote his powerful *An Appeal to the Religion, Justice and Humanity of the Inhabitants of the British Empire on behalf of the Negro Slaves in the West Indies* in 1823. Though leadership was now handed over to Thomas Fowell Buxton, Wilberforce was still an influential figure. Eventually success came, and slavery was abolished. There were those who felt that the compensation to the West Indian slave owners had been far too generous. But as Wilberforce himself famously said on 25 July 1833, the day the second and decisive reading of the Bill was passed, 'Thank God that I should have lived to witness a day in which England is willing to give twenty millions sterling for the Abolition of Slavery.'

Wilberforce and his fellow campaigners had always believed in particular Providence, and the fact that he died a few days later on 29 July seemed then, and seems now, a singular mark of the way in which Providence signalled that a particular commission had been fulfilled. 'It is', as Buxton put it, 'a singular fact that on the very night on which we successfully engaged in the House of Commons, in passing the clause of the Act of Emancipation – one of the most important clauses ever enacted ... the spirit of our friend left the world. The day which saw the termination of his labours saw also the termination of his life.'[46]

The story of the abolition of slavery is moving and powerful because it shows particular individuals persuading a particular country to put a moral cause before self-interest. It shows that these individuals were motivated by their religious principles. These principles pointed to the positive effects of acting appropriately. They also pointed to the negative effects of acting inappropriately. Of course there were other factors which favoured their cause, though they are much more obvious with hindsight than they were at the time, when the odds seemed stacked very heavily against them. Subsequent historians have sometimes exaggerated these factors to the point where the vision, courage, persistence and faith of the individuals have been minimised and obscured.

It is fitting that in the 200th anniversary year of the successful end of the first campaign (at the time of writing), we recall also the power that moral and religious principles had when taken up by committed people who were prepared to act in the world. They served in this way because they were convinced that God had given them a purpose which was to work for the good of others, even when there was no obvious consequential gain to themselves – save that of knowing that they had done what was right by bringing to an end a system that was wrong. The parallels to the needs of our own day are many and obvious, but that is another story.

CHAPTER 8

CHRISTIANS AND MUSLIMS IN BRITAIN

SHUSHA GUPPY

'You will find that... the nearest in affection to you (the faithful) are those who say: "We are Christians". That is because there are priests and monks among them; and because they are free from arrogance.' The Quran, 5/82.

This is one of several references in the Quran to the affinity between Christians and Muslims. As a young man accompanying the caravans of merchandise to Syria, the Prophet met and was befriended by Christian monks, notably Bahira, a Nestorian monk whom he met in 581 in Bosra. It is reported in chronicles that, impressed by his intellectual precocity, and seeing 'the seal of Prophesy between his shoulders', the monk predicted a radiant future for him. In subsequent journeys young Mohammad visited Bahira and studied with him. After the advent of Islam, Bosra was held in esteem and affection by Muslims and became an important stop on the pilgrims' road to Mecca. Vestiges of Bahira's monastery remain, and today's travellers are led to them by guides.

It is certain that the Prophet had a special affection for Christ – He is mentioned repeatedly as 'God's Beloved' in the Quran, and a whole *Sura* (chapter) is devoted to His Mother. One can say that the cult of the Virgin was promoted by Islam. Yet the relationship between the Islamic world and Christendom has fluctuated throughout history. At its zenith, for example in Moorish Spain from the seventh to the 14th centuries in Andalusia, the kingdom of Granada and Toledo, Muslim, Jewish and Christian savants and philosophers working together in harmony led to the flowering of the Renaissance. It came to an end with the expulsion of Jews and

Muslims by Isabella and Ferdinand, which set off the slow decline of the Spanish empire.

In recent history there was a rapprochement between the Islamic world and Christianity, in particular the Catholic Church, during the pontificate of the much maligned but saintly and intellectually sound Pope Pius XII. Their common enemies were growing atheism and aggressive godless Communism. When I was a student in Paris towards the end of the 1950s, one of our professors, the renowned philosopher and Islamic scholar Louis Massignon, had tried to persuade Pope Pius XII to canonise Hallaj, the eighth-century Sufi martyr, who was burnt in Baghdad for his mystical writings. The Pope was pondering the matter when he died.[1] But during his pontificate he was well disposed towards the Muslims: 'Don't be hard on Muslims', he is reported to have said to his Cardinals, 'Remember that over one billion men and women prostrate themselves before God every day.'[2]

Great religious traditions are the expressions of the perennial wisdom which is the ground of civilisation. The atheist 'scientist' West may reject religion, but it is still living off the spiritual and moral *credit* of Christianity – God help it if the credit runs out. Similarly the agnostic Muslim, who denies or rejects his religion, still draws on its precepts and principles. Fundamentalism is the mortal enemy of religion, whether Jewish, Christian, Hindu or Muslim. But so-called Islamic Fundamentalism in its present virulent form seems particularly lethal. It is important to diagnose and understand the illness in order to find a remedy for it.

*****

There has always been a fundamentalist current in Islam, as in all revealed religions, based on a literal, narrow, unimaginative interpretation of the scriptures. In Islam it goes back to Ibn Hanbal, who lived in eighth-century Baghdad. He was opposed by the Khalif and executed, but his theology, Hanbalism, lay dormant like a virus to erupt from time to time. It surfaced through a new carrier, Ibn Taimyya (1263–1338), in Syria. He preached against philosophy, science, even theology, and was finally killed. Soon he was forgotten as 'the mad mullah', but his doctrine surfaced through Mohammad bin Abdul Wahhab (1703–92). This time, instead of disappearing without trace, it spread in the Arabian Peninsula, and was embraced by Ib Saud, the founder of the Kingdom of Saudi Arabia, who made Wahhabism the state religion of the new country, and imposed it ruthlessly. Far from being 'fundamental', Wahhabism is a form of superstitious primitivism which is rejected by the serious Islamic Ulama everywhere. Unfortunately oil was discovered in Saudi Arabia, and some of the petrodollars it generated – what remained after the profligacy of the dictatorial Saudi ruling clan, money burnt on useless arms, Western casinos and tall blondes – was spent in propagating Wahhabism across the world, especially among the poor and disenfranchised Muslims.

It found an echo among some Muslims because of the decline of their societies which made them vulnerable to colonial aggression. Muslims had been promised victory over their enemies as long as they remained faithful and virtuous, which had been the case for centuries. When they began to lose their sovereignty to Western powers, starting with the shock of Napoleon's conquest of Egypt, they were bewildered, wondering if it was not a punishment for their deviation from the simple, original Islam of the Prophet and his early successors.

Wahabbism declares all other religions, and Islamic creeds such as Shiism and Ismailism, *Kufr* – heresy – and their adherents *Kuffar,* heretics, whose punishment is death and their killing lawful. To this day Sufism, the mystical heart of Islam, is forbidden in Saudi Arabia, and even theology is a banned subject of study. Nothing could be further from both the letter and the spirit of Islam, whose compassion, tolerance and acceptance of others are embedded in its scripture. Had Islam contained such 'laws' it would not have survived more than a few decades – how long did Communism last? How long Nazism? Instead, Islam spread throughout the world, and produced one of the most splendid flowerings of the human spirit in history – in science, architecture, the arts, music, poetry and literature. Listening to Persian classical music on a trip to Iran, the late Yehudi Menuhin was moved to say: 'This music is a ladder between the soul and God.' 'By their fruit shall ye know them.'

There are many verses in the Quran asserting the voluntary nature of religion: 'There is no compulsion in religion', is the most quoted (2/256). All revealed religions are accepted and revered; only 'idol-worship' is condemned. Today when idol worship is pervasive – money, fame, film and sport stars, and even dead princesses – the interdict seems pertinent.

Contrary to received wisdom, Islam was not 'imposed by the sword' but spread mostly through voluntary conversion – in Iran it took 600 years before the whole country was converted. Rather it was Islam's ecumenical, universalist message of Unity, its core principles of mercy, compassion, justice and love that appealed. In India conversion was mostly through the influence of wandering Sufis who preached the 'religion of Love', celebrated by the poetry of such great poets as Attar, Rumi, Hafiz, Saadi, Amir Khosrow, and many more. These principles enabled people of different religions – Jews, Christians, Zoroastrians, Hindus and others – to live together in peace and to cooperate for the good of humankind.

We are now at the nadir of Christian-Islamic relations. Since September 11, Islam has become almost synonymous with terrorism, and Muslims of all denominations identified with a few terrorists. It is as if the entire culture of Japan, its Buddhist and Shintoist spiritual heritage, was dismissed because of a few kamikazes.

Although the Arabs constitute less than one-fifth of Muslims, of whom only some five million live in Saudi Arabia – in the abode of Islam (*dar al-Islam)* there are many mansions – in anti-Islam propaganda the Muslim is always a Saudi Arab, dressed in flowing robes and *Kafia* (headscarf fastened with a twisted rope) – and looks like the Jew in Nazi posters – ugly, shifty, lascivious, greedy. Muslims have become the Jews *de nos jours*. The fact that the terrorists are not representative, that the overwhelming majority of their victims are Muslims, that Islam is what 1.3 billion Muslims, from China and Australia to Africa, Europe and America live by daily, does not seem to count – the body is blamed for the disease. There is talk of a 'clash of civilisations', and Islam has replaced Communism as the ultimate enemy.

How have we arrived at this pass?

*****

In an interview to the French weekly *Le Nouvel Observateur,* President Carter's advisor Zbigniew Brzezinski confessed that he had 'engineered' the invasion of Afghanistan by the Soviet Union through 'a feint', in order to create 'a Vietnam for the Russians'. The Afghan resistance movement was duly backed by America, through its 'clients' – Pakistan and Saudi Arabia, the former providing practical military assistance and intelligence, the latter finance. When after ten years of war the Russians were defeated, America, having achieved its purpose, 'dropped Afghanistan' (in the despairing words of Ahmad Shah Massud, the heroic leader of the Mujahedins, shortly before his assassination by Al Qaeda), and handed it over to Saudi Arabia and Pakistan, who unleashed the Taliban, whom they had created like a deadly venom in a laboratory, upon it. We have been living with the consequences ever since. Yet Brzezinski was unrepentant: 'what is more important', he asked the interviewer, 'the collapse of the Soviet Union or the Taliban?' September 11 changed such heartless complacency.

Apart from Afghanistan, 'the Brzezinski doctrine' proposed the creation of a 'green belt' around the Soviet Union – green being the colour of Islam – in Central Asia and the Balkans, particularly after the fall of the Shah, when the equilibrium he had maintained in the Middle East was broken. Saudi Arabia, fearful of the revival of Shia Islam in the Middle East, especially among its own Shia population, who live largely in the oil-rich southern area of the country and are its poorest and most down-trodden citizens, began feverishly building mosques and *madrasas* (religious schools) all over the world, including in Britain, and entrusting them to phoney, ignorant, often psychopathic 'sheikhs' and 'imams' – such as the notorious Abu Hamza of the Finsbury Park mosque, a favourite of our media – to preach Wahhabi dogmatism and propagate hatred. Ismail Kadare, the great Albanian writer (winner of the International Booker Prize 2005), told me that in Macedonia alone the Saudis had built some 500 mosques, but 'not a single hospital, hospice, school, road...' Still our governments did nothing to stop the spread of the poison in Britain. Only after the suicide-bomb attacks of 7 July 2005 did they wake up to reality.

Ironically, the Saudi ruling class themselves have realised that the Frankenstein they have created has got out of hand and has turned against them: Osama Bin Laden has declared war on the rulers of his country, accusing them of laxity. I do not know a single Saudi who does not denounce Wahhabism, or curse it for what it has spawned: 'If Wahhabism is not stopped, it will destroy Islam', a Saudi university professor recently told me. King Abdallah, by all accounts a better and wiser ruler, is trying to turn the tide by introducing a measure of democracy and finding a solution for the Israel-Palestine conflict. If he succeeds he may salvage something.

*****

One of the more nefarious by-products of 9/11 has been the emergence of mountains of books and articles on Islam by self-appointed 'experts' in the West. Individuals who know nothing about Islam, its doctrine, theology and history, and who have never set foot in an Islamic country or visited a Muslim home, hold forth peremptorily about Islam. Suddenly everybody is an 'authority' on the Quran, spouting a few words taken out of context, from dodgy translations – most *de luxe* editions of the Quran sold cheaply, or given away freely, in this country are produced with Saudi/Wahhabi money – to support their prejudices. In pursuit of their own personal or political agenda, these 'experts' play on the Western public's anxiety about the dangerous 'Other' among them. Words such as *jihad* (holy war), *sharia* (law) and *hijab* (veil), divorced from their original meanings, have become part of everyday discourse, and mention of the 'true Islam' – rational, tolerant, ecumenical and generous – provokes wry smiles. Yet there is a *hadith* (acts and words of the Prophet) which says that it is a grave sin to comment on the Quran without knowledge. A Muslim theologian visiting London last year told *Newsnight* that the 'imams' in British mosques, such as Abu Hamza, 'are nobodies', and that the media have created them by treating them as valid interlocutors in order to discredit Islam.

In February the Channel 4 documentary programme *Dispatches* uncovered the influence of Wahhabism in this country by showing preachers openly condemning integration, British society and democracy, denigrating women, and praising the Taliban and Al-Qaeda for killing the *Kuffars,* including British soldiers. On hearing snippets of the preview I thought it was a play. But the 'sheikhs' and preachers in the documentary turned out to be 'real', mostly black Americans or West Indian 'converts' – illiterate, ignorant, misogynous, brimming with hatred and anger. The man who heckled the Home Secretary John Reid, and was interviewed on radio and television, was revealed as a Jamaican, unemployed and in trouble with the police for alleged drug-pushing, who had suddenly 'converted', grown a beard, donned a long white robe and a head scarf, and declared himself sheikh. He was accompanied by his 'followers', a small group of youngsters looking bored and lost, vacantly listening to his incoherent rant.

*****

The majority of Muslim immigrants in Britain are originally from Pakistan and Bangladesh, and from the poorest and least educated sections of their societies. They came here in search of work and a better life, and we needed them to do the jobs that our own workers were reluctant to take on. There is seldom any problem with the first generation of immigrants, as they usually have chosen to leave their own countries and are happy to have escaped poverty and, often, tyranny. Problems occur with the second and third generations: torn between two cultures, at home in neither, they feel lost and frustrated, prey to demagogues and rogues. Poverty, bad education and lack of hope and purpose aggravate alienation. Far from helping them, demonising Islam exacerbates their sense of 'otherness'. Instead of encouraging integration, the perennial way for the immigrant to achieve well-being and citizenship, self-appointed 'community leaders' and politically correct politicians have fostered separation and enmity in the name of 'multiculturalism'. Those who warned against multiculturalism, when it began to be promoted, as dangerous and wrong were dismissed as right-wing racists. Only now that its consequences have proved disastrous, doubts are beginning to be expressed, often by the same 'community leaders' and politicians who crushed all dissent. Just as for decades the so-called left-wing intellectuals tried to stifle any criticism of the Soviet system, thereby prolonging the misery of the Russian and Eastern European peoples. Without *la trahison des clercs* (the treason of the intellectuals), perhaps the Communist system would have collapsed much sooner.

It is now accepted that multiculturalism does not work, that it leads to fragmentation and social disruption, and that there has to be a cohesive element, a glue, which unites the variety of ethnic groups: the culture of the overwhelming majority of the host country. British society and its legal system are founded on Christian values, however much they may seem to have deviated from them. They are not incompatible with Islam, and Muslims are enjoined to submit to the laws of the society in which they live. In principle there is no reason why Muslims should not feel perfectly at home in a Christian country as they have always done. Integration in the host country and its culture is the *sine qua non* of harmony in a multi-ethnic society. Yet integration does not mean abandoning one's original traditions and beliefs. On the contrary, the more integrated a community, the more its 'difference' can become an asset, and contribute something original and worthwhile to society as a whole. In Britain we see the input of various integrated ethnic groups in commerce and finance, the arts, the media and academe – everywhere the new blood and energy of integrated immigrants bear rich fruit. By contrast, 'multiculturalism' is arid, divides and breeds discord.

In France, where there are some six million Muslims – against our two million – the aim has always been integration, even if not always fully achieved. Immigrants have to comply with the secular, republican principles and laws of France. When the French government decreed that immigrants be expelled if they commit crimes, or that young girls be barred from school if they wear the hijab, some *bien-pensant* 'liberals' protested in the name of human rights. But soon it became apparent that the majority of French citizens, including Muslims, approved of their government's firmness. Why has the British government been so pusillanimous? It is not 'tolerance' to turn a blind eye to 'honour killing', female circumcision, incitement to hatred and to terrorism. It is indifference, lazy *laissez-aller,* and dereliction of duty. Muslim women in particular must be protected from the tyranny of their families and their milieu.

Take the veil. The Quran enjoins both men and women to dress modestly. In Christianity too, modesty is recommended – to this day in Catholic countries such as Spain, women wear a black scarf, a simplified *mantilla*, at Mass. No one can quarrel with that; indeed, looking at our fashion industry today, one wishes that some notion of decorum were introduced in its production, for often what is on offer can be called *la mode bordel* (brothel-wear), with the emphasis on nudity rather than clothing. Nowhere in the Quran, or the *Sharia* or the *hadith*, is there a question of *burgha, niqab, chador,* or any other gruesome movable prison.

I was raised in a traditional, devout family in Iran. My father was an eminent philosopher, professor of philosophy at the university, as well as a theologian, a *Mujtahid* – one who is qualified to interpret the *Sharia* and issue fatwas. When Reza Shah abolished the veil (*chador*) in 1936, some older women of the family came to my father for advice, asking if they should obey the new law or stay at home and never go out again. He said that the chador was not necessary, as long as they dressed modestly, and covered their heads with a scarf. Thereafter my pious mother dressed in elegant loose tunics, with attractive head scarves, while we, the younger generation, did not wear scarves or cover our heads at all; my enlightened father obeyed the injunction of Ali – the Prophet's cousin, the first Imam of the duodecimal Shias and the patron-saint of Sufis and mystics of all hues – who wrote: 'You must bring up your children for their time, not your own.'

On assignment to Senegal some years ago I visited some forests in the south, and deep within their millennial shade I found small communities. Men and women were all naked, save for a tiny *cache-sexe* – a patch covering the sex. Welcoming, inquisitive, humorous, they gathered around me, and in the course of conversation I asked them what religion they practised. They said they were Muslims. 'Do you say your daily prayers naked?' I asked. They laughed at the question – of course they prayed naked. By contrast, in the cities I saw men and women dressed in traditional colourful Senegalese clothes going to the Mosque for Friday prayer. Yet in certain areas of the Persian Gulf and in Afghanistan and Pakistan, women are made to cover themselves completely, for the rare occasions that they are allowed outdoors.

Muslim women in the West who choose 'voluntarily' to wear the *hijab* are simply drawing attention to themselves. Feeling 'different' from, and repelled by, the prevalent images of women they see in the media, they want to say 'Look at me! I am me, and I am modest and dignified.' They know that if they decide to discard their tight scarves they can, at any time – this is a free country. They believe the *hijab* is an assertion of identity, instead of being a symbol of oppression and tyranny as it is in some 'Islamic' countries.

*****

To be fair there are other reasons beside nasty 'imams' and poor education for the 'radicalisation' of *some* Muslims – we must never forget that the overwhelming majority are law-abiding, productive, often very successful citizens who contribute to the wealth and economic vibrancy of the country – the current British foreign policy is one of the most significant. Our servility to the United States, explained in terms of 'the special relationship' and long friendship – but one can be best friends without abject thraldom, as demonstrated in the past by Churchill, Macmillan, Wilson and Mrs Thatcher – the disastrous war in Iraq, the destruction of Afghanistan and the plight of the Palestinians. Everywhere Islam seems besieged and Muslims victimised.

Al-Zawahiri, Osama Bin Laden's lieutenant, has written that it was the ruthless repression of the second Intifada in Palestine that gave Al-Qaeda the impetus for 9/11. Bin Laden himself claims that it was the bombing of Beirut in 1982 and America's unconditional support of Israel that first made him rebel – 'children massacred, houses destroyed'. Nor can we believe that it is our liberty and democratic way of life that motivates him and his ilk: in a broadcast in 2004 he said that if this were the case 'why did we not attack Sweden?' To say this is not to condone terrorism – all terrorist violence is utterly despicable and anti-Islamic. It is to try and understand the poison in order to find its antidote. Fundamentalism thrives on poverty, ignorance, injustice. To eliminate it, we must strive to remove, as far as possible, these ills.

The mixture of ignorance, ill-will and arrogance of some sections of the media and political class makes ordinary Muslims despair. Until the Iraq sectarian clashes, President Bush did not know that there were two branches of Islam, Shia and Sunni, and that in Iraq the Shias constitute the majority, while the Sunnis had always been the rulers. No one told him that democratic elections would naturally benefit the Shia majority, and that the ruling Sunnis would not relish giving up their power. The result is that after 14 centuries of peaceful coexistence, the two communities are now at each other's throats.

Equally important as bad politics is the lack of intellectual and moral rigour in Western societies, particularly in America and Britain – there is still some modicum of steadfastness in

Catholic countries. Any suggestion that there are limits to individual freedom, as the Pope has said, and that self-gratification cannot be a basis for a moral life, provokes accusations of priggishness, intolerance and being 'judgemental'. In a recent UN report of 21 advanced countries, Britain came last as the place where children are happy and can flourish.[3] By contrast we are champions of teenage pregnancies, divorce, under-age drinking, etc... These can't be dismissed, as 'by-products of freedom', something we just have to put up with. Nor is the alternative to decadence totalitarianism, which itself is the product of moral and civic decay, but the recovery of the traditional values which are the foundation of any civilised social organisation.

Having cut off its spiritual and moral moorings, based on its Christian heritage, Britain seems adrift in a dark sea of relativism and laxity. Profitable careers are made in academe and the media from preaching atheism and entropy. This contributes to anxiety and the feeling of alienation, not only among Muslims, but among all those who believe in something other than material gain and temporary pleasure as the basis of a good life. If human beings are no longer made in the image of God but are merely collections of 'selfish genes', with no purpose save survival, why should they not behave selfishly? Why should they be bound by any sense of human solidarity, pity, justice, love? 'Greed is good', and casino-capitalism allows unlimited wealth obtained by any means at hardly any effort. The débâcle of such financial institutions such as Enron, Lloyd's, Hollinger et al, breeds cynicism and contributes to the social malaise of which religious fundamentalism is one outcome.

Our present government must be the first to actively *promote* vice – mega-casinos in every city for round-the-clock gambling, despite warnings by social scientists that it causes addiction, racketeering, gangsterism and other ills attendant upon such establishments. Instead of responsibilities we have countless 'rights'; instead of good governance, unlimited 'choice', instead of piety and restraint, maximum self-indulgence.

*****

What is to be done?

I believe this country must reclaim its Christian values – atheists and agnostics can claim that these are simply humanistic values – and uphold its laws. It must also reclaim its sovereignty in foreign policy and defend the interests of its own people. Only then can it be a good friend of America and an effective partner in the European Community. Only then will Muslims and other religious and ethnic minorities feel at home, safe and participants in the common good.

Then there is the issue of immigration. There are those who advocate unlimited immigration, saying that it is good for the economy, and those who wish to ban it completely. Surely there can be a golden mean: controlled immigration, in proportion to our capacity for absorption and integration. Unbridled immigration has negative social consequences that far outweigh its benefits – in housing, education, health and social harmony. The first victims are the immigrants themselves. Exile is a terrible thing; human beings are not made to be uprooted and people do not wish to leave their homeland except in desperation. If we really feel sorry for the plight of the Africans and Asians knocking at Europe's door, we must help them by not backing corrupt incompetent dictators who are responsible for their misery, and by supporting their efforts to remove them – Zimbabwe is a case in point. Also by fair trading, access to world markets for their produce, properly administered aid and other positive measures. After all we are at least partly responsible for their woes. Those immigrants whom we do accept, and whose labour contributes to our wealth, must be integrated and rewarded.

Integration is achieved when every member of society, regardless of colour, creed or gender, accepts some authority that is above and beyond politics, and which represents the entirety of the nation. In France it is the republican principles derived originally from the Enlightenment; in America it is the allegiance to the constitution; in Britain it is the monarchy. Asked why he was passionately in favour of the monarchy, Winston Churchill is said to have answered, 'Because it separates pomp from politics.' There is truth in the quip. The Queen, with her discreet Christian faith, her experience and wisdom, is an ideal agent of national cohesion. When the Australians voted to keep her as their head of state, a television interviewer asked a man in the street why he had voted for the status quo rather than an independent republic. 'I prefer the Queen to any temporary president', he answered.

The monarchy is what guarantees this country's sovereignty and uniqueness. Those republicans who bay for its demise do not realise that they would deprive the ordinary people of their only true representative and recourse. A recent television programme on Prince Charles, *A Meddling Prince,* attacked the Prince of Wales for allegedly having said something against McDonald's 'Big Mac'. It was a trial by television in which judge, jury and prosecutor were the same, and the verdict of guilty a foregone conclusion. Not a single dissenting voice among the people interviewed – journalists, media pundits, 'personalities'; all condemned him for expressing his opinion. So much for freedom of expression! What kind of trial denies the accused any right to representation or counsel? Why was there no witness for the defence?

In reality the Prince of Wales often expresses the feelings and concerns of the majority of the population, providing a voice for those who have no other. In so doing he exposes himself to a daily deluge of adverse publicity and baseless accusations, instead of opting for a quiet life. Thus he fulfils the traditional role of the king, which is to be on the side of the people against the 'barons'. In the present circumstance this is nothing short of heroic, what the Ancient Wisdom called 'Spiritual Chivalry'. Considering his background and milieu, the Prince's faith and spirituality seem a miracle. When he said that he was 'the keeper of faiths' rather than 'of the Faith' – the Church of England – he was asserting the transcendental unity of religions and the role of the monarch as the representative of the whole community. The Catholics and the Orthodox, as well as the Muslims, the Hindus and the

Sikhs – to mention the most prevalent creeds in Britain – can rely on the Sovereign's protection. He knows that once he becomes king, he will be more circumscribed in expressing his views.

Finally, instead of constantly denigrating Islam because of the minority of misfits, we can encourage and publicise its more spiritual and gentle expressions. The year 2007 has been declared by UNESCO the Year of Rumi, to celebrate the 800th anniversary of the birth of Jalaludin Rumi, the Persian poet who is considered the greatest mystic poet in world literature. He was born in 1207 in Iran and died in Qonia, in southern Turkey, in 1273. He belonged to the branch of Sufism (Islamic mysticism) called the mysticism of Love, in which the emphasis is not so much on the law or doctrinal details as on achieving Unity with the Divine through Love. In recent years Rumi has become very fashionable in the West. He is an all-time bestseller in America, and artists, musicians, writers and poets claim an influence – Leonard Cohen, Philip Glass, Robert Bly, Donna Karen, to name a few famous votaries. Even Madonna in an interview declared that Rumi was her favourite poet, which made the Master not so much spin in his grave as to smile benevolently.

Celebrations are planned for Rumi's anniversary by UNESCO all over the world, especially in Qonia, Turkey, where the poet lived most of his life and is buried. In the course of making a programme for BBC Radio on Rumi, I found many Sufi fraternities and organisations in London – people of all faiths, backgrounds, classes and professions, often gathering in churches, reciting his poetry, playing the music associated with his Order, the Whirling Dervishes. Such ecumenical fraternity and desire for spirituality demonstrate that distrust and bigotry are by no means all-pervasive.

We can do with more programmes on radio and television which put the emphasis on harmony and what unites us in our common humanity and spiritual aspirations rather than that which divides us. There is no 'clash of civilisations', and as Rumi expresses, only Love redeems.

O Love, You who have been called by a thousand names,
You who know how to pour the Wine into the chalice of the soul,
You who give culture to a thousand cultures,
You who are faceless but have a thousand faces,
O Love! You who shape the faces of Turks, Persians and Africans,
Pour me a cup from your Pitcher....
....
If there were no Love, what would be the reason for Being?
Who would have nurtured you, and where would you be?
....
If there were not the pure ocean of Love,
Why would I have created the Universe?
......
Love is that which stuns you,
And lifts you above faith or disbelief.

CHAPTER 9

SHORING UP THE FOUNDATIONS: SUPPORTING TRADITIONAL MARRIAGE AND THE FAMILY?

PHILIPPA TAYLOR

> Marriage should be honoured by all...[1]

> I think people are growing out of marriage.[2]

> We've got to take back the right to speak about the most important institution that man has evolved over thousands of years.[3]

We live in an age where there are increasingly divergent views on how we should regard 'the family'. There is the optimistic view of the family, which sees it developing into a diversity of different forms for couples to choose from, where the basis for a family is any relationship that is perceived as good and caring. Those who hold this view perceive 'the family' as improving, adapting to fit people's individual needs, freeing them from oppressive and dysfunctional relationships. Children are seen as adaptable, resilient and able to cope with different family forms, as long as conflict is relatively well managed.

The more pessimistic view of the family sees it as being under pressure from libertarian and individualistic views. This is evidenced by the development of different family forms, the retreat from marriage and the high rate of relationship breakdown, along with concerns for children's well-being and vulnerability. Those who hold this view are concerned about the undermining of the value of faithful and long-term marriage relationships and believe that because the 'traditional' marriage relationship is so important for the functioning and stability of individuals and society, it needs to be reclaimed and built up.

There are drawbacks to both of these perceptions. Those who hark back to a 'traditional' view of marriage run the risk of forgetting, or under-playing, the sometimes oppressive roles and expectations that both men and women had. This view often ignores today's very different labour market, which enables women, with their increased educational qualifications, to challenge the traditional stereotypical roles of the male breadwinner and the homemaker mother. On the other hand, couple relationships based solely on 'the thin and fragile reed of affection'[4] are markedly more tenuous. Those who expound the more optimistic view of the family can tend to underestimate enduring gender inequalities and domestic violence, as well as the adverse effects of separation on children and adults, and difficulties associated with blended or stepfamilies.

My purpose in this chapter is to try to steer a middle way and suggest how we might bring about a marriage renaissance, by bringing together the best elements of the more 'traditional' understanding of marriage along with the best elements of today's more diverse conceptualisation of relationships, so that 'healthy' marriage becomes the relationship of choice in the future. But first it is important to explore further this diversity and see how marriage has evolved, in order to illuminate what marriage is, how we have got here and where we might head.

HISTORICAL PERSPECTIVES ON MARRIAGE

Marriage is a complex social phenomenon and has been perceived as such throughout history. Far from being unknown in other centuries (or 'invented' in the 1950s) the small unit of two parents plus children is an ancient, widespread and cohesive arrangement. For thousands of years, marriage, or its equivalent, has organised people's places in the economic and political hierarchy of society:

> Throughout humanity's historical and civilisational experience the family has been characterised by constants and variations. The constants are: permanent union of a man and a wife in caring partnership; civic and ritual authorisation and recognition of such partnerships; restriction of legitimate procreation of children to such partnerships; protection of the rights and responsibility of married partners to the rearing of their children.[5]

In 866 Pope Nicholas I said:

> let the simple consent of those whose wedding is in question be sufficient; if the consent be lacking in a marriage, all other celebrations, even should the union be consummated, are rendered void.

Eight hundred years later, Henry Swinburne wrote in his Treatise of Spousals:

> Albeit there be no witnesses of the contract, yet the parties having verily (though secretly) contracted matrimony, they are very man and wife before God. Neither can either of them with safe conscience marry elsewhere so long as the other party liveth.[6]

These two quotes sum up the essence of marriage in this country; it was effected through the freely given consent of both parties and it was indissoluble. Until the 1750s, marriage was largely a private matter between two individuals and their kin. However, although marriages were not binding *without* a public ceremony, they *were* publicly acknowledged because clandestine marriages – those done secretly – were valid in the eyes of the Church and the law. The Hardwicke Marriage Act of 1753 took control over marriage from the hands of individuals and vested it in the state. In other words, it was only in 1754 that a ceremony became a legal requirement in England and Wales for the establishing of a marriage.

Callan[7] notes that it is easy to assume that high rates of cohabitation and non-marriage and the later average age of first marriage are all by-products of modernity. However, these patterns have been evident, though fluctuating, since the 16th century, and rituals[8] show that forms of informal cohabitation have long existed alongside marriage. Themes of individualism can be seen in our culture from as far back as the 14th century. Over the centuries the popularity of marriage has waxed and waned, and there were concerns about marriage levels at the end of the 19th century. We should not observe today's high divorce and cohabitation rates from the vantage point of the recent 1950s but from the last millennium, with a longer-term view.

Nevertheless, historians are concluding that a worldwide transformation of marriage *is* now in the process of taking place. In the words of Coontz, a US family historian:

> Many things that seem new in family life are actually quite traditional ... many societies have had a very casual attitude toward what deserves recognition as a marriage. The "tradition" that marriage has to be licensed by the state or sanctified by the church is more recent than most people assume ... I still believe that when it comes to any particular practice or variation on marriage, there is really nothing new under the sun. But when we look at the larger picture, it is clear that the social role and mutual relationship of marriage, divorce, and singlehood in the contemporary world is qualitatively different from anything to be found in the past. Almost any separate way of organising family life has been tried by some society at some point in time. But the coexistence in one society of so many alternative ways of doing all of these different things – and the comparative legitimacy accorded to many of them – has never been seen before.[9]

Whatever functions marriage served for the man and woman involved and for the children they produced, historically, marriage was not primarily for their individual benefit. It was a way of raising capital, constructing political alliances, organising work, deciding what claims children had on their parents and what rights parents had on their children. Marriage served so many political, social and economic functions that the individual needs and desires of its members were secondary considerations. But this is not to say that love and affection have never been part of marriage. Most people have probably always married at least partly because of prior affection, and we have many written examples that love within marriage has long been valued:

> See now the nature of the contract by which they (the married couple) bind themselves in consented marriage. Henceforth and forever each shall be to the other as a same self in all sincere love, all careful solitude, every kindness of affection, in constant compassion, unflagging consolation and faithful devotedness.[10]

The plurality of relationships that we see today, however, is primarily the consequence of personal lifestyle decisions and attitudes in the area of marriage and family life, whereas in the past, changes were largely the result of 'societal constraints on marriage and family formation and death'.[11] In some ways, the history of marriage can be seen as the growing importance of the unitive values of marriage (affection, sexual relationships etc) alongside the decline of the procreative value of marriage.[12] In other words, there has been a change in emphasis to the primacy of relationship over the objective 'good' of procreation and mutual and nurturing sacrifice. The challenge, if we are to try and hold together the best of the old with the best of the new, is to try and hold both the relational *and* procreational intents together within marriage.

In other words, the unitive and procreative ends of marriage are connected and must stay so, for the benefit of both the couple and their children. I explore the sociological developments within relationships further in the next section.

SOCIOLOGICAL PERSPECTIVES ON MARRIAGE

Two important changes to the meaning of marriage took place during the 20th century.[13] The first change, noted by Burgess, which was making itself felt at the end of the Second World War, was from an 'institution' to a 'companionship' understanding of marriage. This was the single-earner, home-maker marriage of the 1950s. The second transition, which began in the 1960s, was to the 'individualised marriage' in which the emphasis on personal choice and self-development took hold. The roles of wives and husbands became more flexible and open to negotiation, and a more individualistic perspective on the rewards of marriage took root. There was a shift from 'role' to 'self' as people began to focus on their own development, as opposed to simply sacrificing oneself and gaining satisfaction through building a family and playing the roles of spouse and parent.[14]

Sociological theorists have written about the growing individualisation of personal and married life. Giddens in particular popularised the concept of 'pure relationships', which are self-sustaining, needing no support, regulation and constraints by external standards, laws or conventions. These 'pure relationships' (married or not) will continue for as long as the relationship is thought by each individual to deliver enough personal satisfaction. As Cherlin notes, this is the logical extension of the increasing individualism and deinstitutionalisation of marriage that occurred in the late 20th century.[15]

As I said earlier, the focus on love is not a recent discovery. However, as the value of a relationship has become the primary goal now for individual development, self-esteem and personal worth, the pressure has built to constantly review the relationship, and to separate and seek a new partner if the original partner can no longer promote this personal growth and development or fulfil (high) relationship expectations.

Today's 'pure relationship' is set within the private domain. It has become a personal lifestyle choice, set free from public or intergenerational ties, and it sits uneasily with goals of life partnership and self-sacrifice. On the other hand, the breakdown of the old rules of the 'traditional'-gendered institution of marriage has led to the creation of a more equal relationship between wives and husbands and/or partners.[16] Many of the changes in relationships in the late 20th and early 21st centuries have come about from increased opportunities and expectations, particularly for women. Some of the rigid norms that once structured society, constraining choice and opportunity, have now broken down. However, this breakdown of the old structures and roles within the home has brought with it a greater risk of insecurity, conflict and the need for ongoing negotiation between partners if relationships are to survive.

One of the problems with the 'private relationship' is that, Schluter warns,[17] most of us still need to be relationally proximate to other people. If our wider, supporting, networks are weak (through isolation, rootlessness and endless mobility), when the couple-centred marriage dissolves into self-centred marriage, there can be too much pressure on the partners to negotiate and bear the expectations and roles of the other. This becomes dangerous for the relationship as it inevitably leads to disagreement, dissatisfaction and an environment where children become 'objects of sentimental gratification'.[18] Furthermore, somewhat ironically, although liberal ideals state that people must be able to choose freely and privately how they conduct their lives, when families split up then children (and sometimes the primary carer) are often seen as the responsibility of the state and no longer restricted to the private domain.

THE COMPLEXITY OF COMMITMENT

Another of the significant changes in relationship formation has been the blurring of the lines between different types and stages of relationships. Marriage is usually no longer regarded as the start of a relationship but as the final stage, as a relational ideal to aim for. It is 'the prize at the end of the race'.[19] Although the practical importance of marriage has declined this century and the purpose of marriage has changed, its symbolic significance and distinctiveness have remained high and may even have increased. It has become a marker of prestige and personal achievement, something to aspire to.[20] Negatively though, the view of marriage as a relational process has led to it being marginalised because of the perception that it does not matter if couples are married or cohabiting. Instead, what is important are the dynamics of the relationship, its inner workings.

While the terms 'marriage' and 'cohabitation' are still useful in classifying and defining different relationships, their use has tended to polarise opinion in the UK by focusing debate on marriage versus cohabitation. The reality is that these terms hide underlying complexities of commitment within different relationships today. A 'cohabiting couple' can be a couple who have recently moved in together with no long-term plans, or a couple who have lived together for 20 years, have three children and consider their commitment to each other to be rock-solid, the result of a private pact that has come to be socially acknowledged as a result of its demonstrated longevity. And whilst it is easy to assume that people who are married are more committed, within marriage there is some similar complexity; one of the results of the privatisation of, and individualism within, marriage has been to reduce it to little more than an 'affectionate sexual relationship of tentative commitment and uncertain duration'[21] – so many enter it knowing they will walk out if it does not fulfil their expectations or needs.

Sociologists Smart and Stevens[22] have described these different forms of commitment as forming a continuum ranging from 'mutual' to 'contingent' commitment. Mutual commitment is where there is some agreement on what is expected of the relationship and people have a long-term perspective. Contingent commitment is where issues are not resolved and the relationship is maintained out of expediency. At the far end of the mutual commitment range these relationships are marriage-like in that there is some moral commitment (a sense of duty to see things through), and often some structural commitment (in the form of jointly owned property). Contingent commitment is likely to involve largely personal commitment ('what is best for *me*').[23]

Some marriages are characterised by contingent commitment and some cohabitations by mutual commitment, hence the difficulties with terminology. However, although it is inaccurate to treat all cohabitation as essentially short-lived, long-term, committed cohabitation is in reality not that common. The average duration of a cohabiting union is around two years and less than 5 per cent of cohabitations last ten years or more.[24] In contrast, the average length of marriage – ending in divorce or death – is 24 years.[25]

Stanley notes that there can be an inbuilt ambiguity to cohabiting relationships, with one partner more committed than the other because couples often 'slide' into cohabiting without seriously 'deciding' or considering the implications beforehand: 'it just happened'.[26] The difference with marriage is that it begins with a clear public and legal declaration of life-long commitment:

> The crucial point is that for a married couple, whatever their private thoughts and perhaps conflicting emotions and expectations, there lies behind them a public, explicit and unconditional commitment of each to the other for life.[27]

Cohabitation, in contrast, requires only a private commitment, which is easier to break.

JUDAEO-CHRISTIAN PERSPECTIVES OF MARRIAGE

The concept of marriage, and its associated ceremony, varies in different cultures and in different legal systems. However, some form or concept of marriage[28] has been found to exist in all human societies, past and present. For example, Jews, Buddhists, Muslims and Hindus, as well as Christians, have all recognised lifelong, committed unions that are legalised or formalised within their individual cultures.

> The theory of marriage in the West has had a religious dimension, but beneath and within the symbolism of religion can be found a variety of additional features. One can find naturalistic assumptions about human nature; Greek, Roman and German legal theories about marriage; and philosophical perspectives from Plato, Aristotle, Kant, Locke and Rousseau.[29]

Western practices have been particularly shaped by the Judaeo-Christian understanding of marriage, based on the account of creation in the Bible:

> ... At the beginning the Creator "made them male and female ... for this reason a man will leave his father and mother and be united to his wife, and the two will become one flesh". So they are no longer two, but one. Therefore what God has joined together, let man not separate.[30]

These few words establish the essential ingredients of marriage: a lifelong commitment between a man and a woman that is publicly made. Though this relationship is upset by the Fall described in Genesis, it is clearly set down as the ideal model of male-female relationships for all time. These essentials are also part of secular marriage law in Britain today.[31] The Genesis text illustrates three of the 'legs' that marriage stands on: leaving, cleaving and 'one flesh'. Leaving points to the establishment of a new family and social unit; cleaving[32] points to the committed faithfulness that one promises to the other; and 'one flesh' points to the personal union, the oneness of man and woman. The primary purpose of human sexual relationship is this unitive relationship between the partners, but a further purpose is the procreative one of building a family. The two belong together in the biblical understanding of marriage.[33]

Marriage is also described in the Bible as a covenant relationship, witnessed by God.[34] A covenant is a social, public and legal agreement, with terms and promises that are made between each party and before witnesses. Unlike a contract, a covenant is not open to periodic negotiation according to the desires of the parties. Because the marriage covenant, established by binding vows, is witnessed by others, the public dimension is at the heart of marriage. Some authors have suggested that cohabitation is the modern-day equivalent of the historical practice of 'betrothal', but the all-important social and public dimension of betrothal is lacking from the practice of cohabitation today. Indeed, a haze of ambiguity surrounds most cohabitating relationships. They often begin in a private and casual way – the couple does not clearly discuss and agree on the type and depth of commitment to each other – so the precise nature of their relationship is undefined. There is not usually any secret that a couple is living together, but to those around, the exact meaning and status of the relationship are unclear. This is because cohabitation, unlike marriage, is essentially a private agreement between two individuals. In this respect, it falls short of the considered, well-defined, public commitment that biblical and secular marriage requires.

In so far as there is usually no commitment to permanence in a cohabiting relationship, it again can fall short of biblical norms 'what God has joined together, let man not separate'. However, as I noted earlier, no two cohabiting relationships are exactly alike, thus we need to evaluate the extent to which different types of cohabiting relationships fall short of, or fall within, these standards. In the same way, and despite the clearer parameters for marriage, there is diversity within marriages too, and individual marriages can also fall short of a commitment to permanence and exclusivity. It may be that judging whether a cohabiting relationship is actually a marriage, or whether a marriage is really a biblical marriage, can only be done after a long period of time has revealed the reality of the relationship.

The Judaeo-Christian belief is that God has created us and our capacity and purpose for relationship, therefore marriage is not a human invention but is an innate and inescapable part of our human nature. The universality of marriage within different cultures and societies and over time indicates that marriage is a divinely ordained ordinance, not just an invention, a construct of human will, nor a particular phase in social evolution, as claimed by some sociologists. Marriage cannot be '*an item of cultural history, in a process of constant metamorphosis*' because '*Created order is not negotiable within the course of history*'.[35] Thus experiments to try and reconstruct or extinguish the marriage bond will fail because the need and desire for the special pair-bonding of marriage will always be there, and we can never develop beyond the need for it.

O'Donovan states that marriage will be with us, in one form or another, as a 'natural good' until the kingdom of God appears.[36] Part of the importance of understanding the Judaeo-Christian perspectives of marriage, and its grounding in creation, is to reveal the many similar elements with secular naturalistic assumptions on marriage. Like the philosophers before them, Luther and Calvin argued that marriage was a natural condition subject to natural law, thus some (secondary) Christian principles of marriage applied only to those individuals whose consciences directed them to live this way. This has a high degree of relevance today. We cannot expect people to get married because it is the 'right thing to do'; we have to appeal to natural law, principles which hold true because of our human condition and not because of any moral imperative. Indeed, the close identification of marriage with organised religion is disadvantageous – people resent the Church having any control over their lives when they do not adhere to any of its defining principles.

> So when as Christians we seek to persuade society about this moral order we are not defending the institution of marriage as though the God-given institution of marriage were under ontological threat ... it is not within the power of humankind to finally destroy created order. No Christian movement needs to defend marriage: rather we seek to protect humans against the

> damage done to them by cutting across the grain of the order of marriage. That knowledge takes a burden off our shoulders.[37]

THE BENEFITS OF MARRIAGE

The 'natural good' of marriage can be clearly seen in the wider benefits that it brings to society, as well as the personal benefits which social scientists have identified that marriage brings:

> A new branch of research is finding that marriage has powerful and beneficial effects on human beings ... its findings deserve to be read by everyone in Western society.[38]

The personal benefits have been well documented:

> The emotional support and monitoring of a spouse encourages healthy behaviour that in turn affects emotional as well as physical well-being: regular sleep, a healthy diet, moderate drinking. But the key seems to be the marriage bond itself: having a partner who is committed for better for worse, in sickness and in health, makes people happier and healthier.[39]

A lasting marriage brings as much happiness as having an additional £60,000 income, the economist Oswald has found.[40] He also notes that marriage has a large effect on mortality risk:

> There is remarkable evidence that marriage helps to keep human beings alive ... Evidence for this is now widespread across the world.[41]

Health also is improved by marriage, particularly a good one. These findings have caused Oswald to conclude that:

> Marriage causes a physiological benefit that enhances mental and physical well-being and helps to prolong life ...exactly how marriage works its magic remains mysterious.[42]

Marriage is still highly popular; three-quarters of today's young adults will marry at some stage and 85 per cent of all Britain's couples are married.[43] An academic study initiated by Care for the Family reported that participants felt that being married was an important part of their life and identity, but society in general did not value marriage to the same extent as they did. Marriage was perceived as an act of great symbolic importance and a public statement of commitment.[44]

Healthy marriage provides the most stable and enduring environment in which to nurture children, which I explore further in the next section. It is also the most committed relationship within which to share the support and care for dependent, elderly and disabled adults. Indeed, it is one of the best structures for social security that we have. When relationships break up the impact extends into the social sphere and the public purse: Mr and Mrs Average Married pay over £5000 a year more in tax than they receive in benefits, but if they break up the two households can receive £7000 a year more in benefits than they pay in tax.[45]

THE IMPACT OF FAMILY BREAKDOWN

Family structure cannot be ignored, in terms of outcomes, when we look at relationship breakdown. The Institute for Public Policy Research has recently admitted that:

> Much recent US research reports a consistent overarching finding that children who grow up in an "intact, two-parent family" with both biological parents do better on a wide range of outcomes than children who grow up in a single-parent family. While this research may be instinctively difficult for those on the Left to accept, the British evidence seems to support it.[46]

Again, though, we have to ask does being in a marriage make a difference here or do all 'intact two-parent families' have the same outcomes for children? Callan states:

> So marriage is changing, marriage might eventually evolve out of all recognition. Why does that matter? I think the main reason it matters is because if commitment goes out with marriage then children are more likely to grow up without one of their parents, the idea that you can rely on one person for life would become completely discredited. There would be an expectation of fragility.[47]

Interestingly, when we look at the UK statistics we find that divorce rates are actually dropping, and what is really driving up the numbers of children growing up in divided families is high levels of child-bearing within cohabiting partnerships, *not* marriage. In fact, the breakdown rate of marriages with children under five has actually *declined* between 1991 and 2003.[48] Figures from the Millennium Cohort Study of mothers with three-year-olds found that children of cohabiting parents are 3.5 times more likely to experience family breakdown than if their parents are married.[49] The risk is 13 times greater for those who describe themselves as 'closely involved'. In other words, the majority of family breakdowns affecting young children involves unmarried parents.[50]

The risk of family breakdown is independently influenced by many factors, including both income *and* marital status. My concern is that there is an overemphasis (by government and others) on the influence of financial factors, whereas this recent data shows that marital status actually has the greater influence: the difference in family breakdown risk between married and cohabiting couples is sufficient that even the poorest 20 per cent of married couples are more stable than all but the richest 20 per cent of cohabiting couples.[51]

The reason this matters is the effect of family breakdown on children. As Whitehead says:

> In a culture of divorce, children are the most "unfree".[52]

Marquardt's study of children of divorce found that even the most amicable separations leave long-term effects on children, particularly when they enter their own relationships.[53] The report 'Fractured Families'[54] documents the effects of family breakdown – it is consistently associated with a range of poorer outcomes for both adults and children, such as risks of crime, health problems and family breakdown amongst both children and grandchildren.[55] But importantly, family breakdown is closely linked to child poverty:

> The BHPS analysis shows that ...The rise in cohabitation is implicated in the increasing prevalence of lone parenthood and hence in the growth of child poverty.[56]

And:

> It is well known that one-parent families have an exceptionally high risk of poverty; less well known that the risk is if anything even higher for children whose parents are cohabiting.[57]

Family breakdown is not an issue that adversely affects just children, it affects women too. As marriage has become one of many options, and cohabitation and single parenthood have been 'sold' as 'freedom', campaigners for women's rights should be increasingly concerned about the close connection between cohabiting partnerships and lone parenthood. As de Waal comments,[58] the real problem now is that what distinguishes cohabiting households from married ones is stability, not an equal division of housework. In the past 30 years, the number of both cohabiting and lone-parent families has rocketed ... simultaneously. So while cohabitation is being sold as freedom, its inherent fragility has actually led to a new form of women's 'enslavement':

> That women can today parent alone, and unstigmatised, is a success for women's campaigners, but this is blighted by the reality of lone motherhood. While some middle-class single mothers are having a ball, they're the minority. There's nothing empowering about being left, penniless, holding the baby. Around half of lone mothers have no earned income and scrape by on benefits. Of those who aren't officially poor, many have to do the jobs of two people.[59]

Statistics show that cohabitation was more common among educated women born in the 1950s and 1960s, but the less educated had caught up by the 1970s cohort. Similarly, while the more educated women born in the 1950s and 1960s married later, by the 1970s cohort it was the less educated who married later. And as the rate of cohabitation breakdown has increased over time, it is the less educated who are now more likely to see their union break down than the more educated: 'Less educated women are more likely to have a child outside of a live-in partnership, have a child within a cohabiting union, dissolve a cohabiting union and dissolve a marriage.'[60] The gap between the two groups continues to widen.

Edin and Kefalas, in a study of a poor neighbourhood in the USA, also identified this 'marriage gap' between different income groups. Marriage is a sought-after but elusive goal:

> Once marriage became optional, low-income women lost a culture that told them the truth about what was best for their children. A number of researchers argue that, in fact, low-income women really do want to marry. They have "white picket fence dreams"... and they gaze longingly into the distance at marriage as a

> symbol of middle-class stability and comfort. What they don't have, however, is a clue about the very fact that orders the lives of their more fortunate peers: marriage and childbearing belong together. The result is separate and unequal families, now and as far as the eye can see.[61]

In the UK, Shaun Bailey, who grew up on a council estate, makes a similar observation about the aspirations of low-income families:

> ...government policy...discourages them from raising their children in nuclear families ... if you have to be estranged from the father of your child in order to survive financially, there's a problem. If you talk to young people, most of them support marriage. There are very few who say they wouldn't like to get married, especially the young women.[62]

Family breakdown is not just about children and women; the involvement of fathers also plays a major role in outcomes between the children of married and lone-parent families. It is widely acknowledged that father involvement is associated with better outcomes for children, such as behavioural outcomes, school attendance and higher educational expectations.[63] Conversely, children living without their biological fathers are more likely to experience adverse outcomes: poverty and deprivation, emotional, mental or health problems, risk of emotional or physical abuse, social exclusion, and to repeat the cycle again in the next generation.[64]

The US 'Fragile Families Study' gives some signs of hope, however.[65] It found a high level of father involvement at birth for their child *and* high levels of partner commitment: 83 per cent of parents were romantically involved at birth and over 50 per cent of these were living together. Only 9 per cent of parents had little or no contact with one another. Most unwed fathers were providing financial and other support during the pregnancy and were planning to help raise the child. However, the survey found that relationships were grounded in 'high hopes' but 'low capacities'. Despite hopes for a future together, they face many barriers due to their low capacities. Few parents had married by the time of their child's fifth birthday; instead, break-up rates were high, just as the UK Millennium Cohort findings mentioned earlier found.[66] Again, in contrast, both studies showed that break-up rates for married couples were much lower, less than 10 per cent. Family structure, with these fragile families, does matter.

CAN GOVERNMENT SHORE UP THE FOUNDATIONS?

There is an apocryphal story about a high cliff in a distant city where many vehicles burst through the railings and fell down the cliff. Many people were hurt. The city council voted to have an ambulance always stationed at the foot of the cliff to rescue victims. Little or no effort was made to ensure the railings were strengthened to prevent such accidents, or to provide signs to warn drivers, and the road was not broadened to make it safer. This story parallels the way in which the problems with family breakdown in society today have been dealt with in Western society. Money is poured into dealing with the effects of breakdown (£680–£820 a year per taxpayer), while next to nothing is spent on trying to prevent it in the first place (58p a year).[67]

Despite the obvious complexity of these issues, we do have a way to break down the (often unproductive) debate about marriage versus cohabitation through a better understanding of the continuum of commitment and the diversity of commitment within both cohabitations and marriages. By focusing on bolstering *commitment*, we can and should support all who are in committed relationships. Outcomes for children are so much better when two parents are there for the duration.

But at the same time we must be unapologetic about the fact that *healthy* marriage[68] (high in mutual commitment) provides the best-proven foundation for the family, and therefore must be both given practical encouragement and be well supported from prevailing cultural messages.

The maintenance of a relationship is not the private concern of the couple alone, and the public and private spheres are not insulated from each other. The social context can support or weaken relationships. We need to be careful to refer to correlations rather than causality, but undoubtedly the law, education, employment, housing, tax and benefits, child support and the media have had an impact.[69] Therefore, the Government should actively support healthy marriages through their policies, not shy away from being explicit about the associated benefits for fear of offending people in different family forms. It is not to the long-term benefit of children and parents to claim that family structure is irrelevant and that 'all kinds of families deserve support'. This ignores the fact that some family types bring *on average* more benefits than other family types. Instead, it is 'people in all kinds of families that deserve support'.[70] It is not impossible to support both healthy marriage and all those needing assistance.

Present government efforts are centred on the welcome goal of reducing child poverty, but at the same time the explicit promotion of healthy marriage is widely considered to be political suicide. The majority view is that policies have to reflect the diversity of family formations in the UK today, without promoting one model over another. However, at times this reluctance to adjudicate between different types of relationship has resulted in 'dissent in government and incoherence in policy'.[71] The policy has therefore shifted uneasily between promoting marriage and decrying a judgemental approach. What Durham refers to as 'the balancing act' has drawn fire from all sides. Fearful of losing the support of middle England, the present government has created a family policy that is both ambitious and ambiguous, but its ultimate refusal to 'discriminate' in favour of marriage has made it a target for family values campaigners and others:[72]

> It is a sad fact that a government which has published excellent proposals on helping parents and children after breakdown of relationships has done nothing practical to support married couples. [This] change

of direction away from the support of marriage has created a wasted opportunity to support a section of the public whose value to society has been seriously undervalued.[73]

I suggest four opportunities for the Government to support healthy marriages and commitment in the UK. First, there is a need for more government support for primary relationship intervention, such as preparation and relationship support, because, arguably, the vast majority of family breakdown is avoidable. The 'fragile families' research mentioned earlier recommends that policies and programmes should facilitate, build upon and try to maintain the commitment that unmarried fathers articulate around their child's birth. Programmes designed to improve relationship skills among low-income couples have been found to work and are likely to increase union stability and child well-being, as long as they are tailored appropriately.[74] However, any practical interventions have more chance of success if they are preventative and at the 'right' time – or 'magic moment' – such as before, at or soon after the point of birth, because the break-up rate of these new parents is very high during the first few years of a child's life. The research also found good levels of participation in the marriage programmes, especially if offered these services while there are high hopes for the relationship and the raising of the child together. In fact, the early years of all marriages, not just 'fragile families', are the most vulnerable to separation, so prevention measures and early intervention will be universally appropriate. Voluntary organisations in the UK are already delivering community-based relationship education and have a wealth of experience in teaching communication skills and skills to strengthen relationships, but they require far greater resourcing to be able to reach more people and change communities.

Second, the fragile families survey shows the importance of father involvement, which is possibly one of the most fruitful areas for policy. In the USA the issue of fatherlessness has been used to great effect as a way of encouraging healthy marriage. They have taken on board the extent to which it drives many undesirable social trends such as high rates of teenage pregnancy, youth crime and substance abuse. In the UK we need to similarly adjust the terms of the debate on the family by drawing attention to the separation of parenting from marriage and the consequences of fatherlessness. Again, appropriate intervention and support in the early stages of the relationship, or around the 'magic' point of birth, are key to success.

A third part of the solution is through our current financial legislation because:

> Taxation is not wholly neutral in the way it raises revenue ... how and what is taxed sends clear signals about the ... values (governments) wish to entrench in society.[75]

CARE has for many years campaigned for the Government to give greater support for married, and long-term stable couples, through the tax system.[76] They have argued that as tax credits stand today, many couples are actually *worse off* living together. The cost in terms of lost credits and benefits from living together may well be of the order of £7000 per year. It is implausible that costs of this magnitude are not having an effect on decisions on whether to live together or live apart. Indeed, this may be partly why the numbers of adults 'living-apart together' has increased.[77] Getting tax credits right for couples will also impact on lone parents and their children because the high financial cost involved for couples with children, if they marry or even cohabit, seems likely to be trapping many lone parents into lone parenthood. The more fragile the family, the more likely it is that family life is being affected by these income differentials. This urgently needs to be rectified and CARE has suggested various ways to do so.[78]

The fourth part of the solution is for increasing cultural support for marriage. The evidence I have cited suggests that increasing relationship skills is likely to have a small, but significant, effect on marriage; however, the reality is that changing attitudes towards marriage and long-term committed relationships would make the effect even larger. In other words, we must not ignore the effect of promoting marriage per se, as well as specific relationship skills programmes. The challenge is how we (the Government, media, educators and local communities) might better pull the *cultural* levers – not just economic, rational ones – to raise the cultural acceptability of marriage and commitment, so that people aspire to commit themselves within healthy marriage. A particular challenge is to engage with today's young adults, who desire both friendships and committed relationships but are consumer-orientated in their jobs and relationships, as well as increasingly debt-ridden and cynical.[79]

A simplistic view of marriage which ignores the presence of diversity, as I've outlined above, is not to be recommended. We should be careful about the use of the term 'traditional marriage' because its meaning is not always clear – to some it may mean a certain gender arrangement with mothers at home and fathers in the workforce, whereas to others a simple reference to permanence. Like many others, I see no reason why we should not witness a marriage renaissance, a realignment towards something new that has elements of the past, especially commitment and stability, but also new features such as gender equality and relationship primacy, which weren't the characteristics of the marriages of our past. We should be encouraged that although people have rejected the institutional view of marriage, they do still want to marry, and the symbolic and distinctive significance of marriage remains high. Our challenge therefore is not so much to defend institutional marriage; rather, it is to protect humans against the damage done to them by 'cutting across the grain of the order of marriage'.[80]

Our aim should be to create a cultural and social context that encourages people to aspire to and *choose* to make long-term relationships, high in mutual commitment and equality, ideally within marriage. Then when people choose this, they should be fully supported in their aspirations, practically, socially, culturally and financially. Society will be the better for it.

CHAPTER 10

TO TEACH OR NOT TO TEACH

JOHN MARKS

I will start with three cameos to illustrate what can happen in our schools today.

1. VICTORIAN VALUES IN THE CLASSROM

The first is an extract from one of John Clare's weekly question and answer columns when he was education correspondent of the *Daily Telegraph*:

> Q. I have recently begun collecting my nine-year-old granddaughter from school and have been astonished to discover that the children spend most of their lessons sitting around tables in groups of five or six. It follows that at least half of them are likely to have their backs to their teacher for at least half the time. How on earth do they learn?
>
> A. Very good question. What strikes me as I go round primary schools is how much time pupils spend gossiping to each other or looking distracted while they wait for the teacher to come to their table. I am also disturbed by the time they spend sitting huddled on the floor at their teacher's feet – a consequence of the introduction of literacy and numeracy hours for periods of 'whole-class' teaching. Because their chairs are arranged around half a dozen tables, it is only by sitting on the floor that they are all able to face in the same direction.
>
> Interestingly, a study just published by academics at Nottingham Trent University suggests that this practice,

> almost universal in primary schools, 'makes learning unnecessarily difficult for most of the time'. The researchers seem to have stumbled across the conclusion while watching a teacher engaged in a project on 'the Victorians' with a class of children aged eight and nine. She rearranged the chairs and tables into rows so that they could experience what school was like for their great-grandparents. I cannot do better than quote the publisher's explanation of what happened next. 'She soon began to notice that her children responded in ways she had not anticipated. In both class teaching and individual work, the children were less distracted, and concentration was better than usual. Struck by the difference these changes made, she continued using row arrangements for some activities beyond the end of the project and found the effects endured.' In other words, the children's work improved and so did their behaviour.[1]

2. BACK TO THE FUTURE AGAIN?

The second cameo concerns a chance meeting I had with a friend – an experienced primary school teacher in her 60s – who was working as a supply teacher in a school in one of the shire counties.

I asked how it was going and she told me that the school was being renovated, which meant that she had to teach her class in a portakabin on the far side of the school playing field. 'That must be a problem', I said. 'Oh no', she said, 'It was marvellous!' 'Why?' I asked.

The answer was that because the portakabin was well separated from the rest of the school, she could do as she liked in her classroom. So, like the teachers in cameo 1, she gave up organising her class into half a dozen groups around tables. Instead, she arranged the desks in rows – with all pupils facing the front – and, for most of the time, taught the whole class at once – just as she had done when she started teaching in the mid-1950s.

Just like the teachers in the 'Victorian classroom' in cameo 1, she found that discipline, concentration and work all improved, and teaching and learning were much easier to achieve and were also more fun.

'Couldn't you have done that in the main school building?' I asked.

The answer was categorically no. There you were in full view of the rest of the school and an old-fashioned (Victorian?) classroom would have been frowned upon and strongly discouraged – especially from a supply teacher.

Her closing words to me were: 'I'm dreading next term when the renovations are finished and I have to move back into the main building!'

3. DIDACTIC TEACHING

The third cameo concerns my surprise when I read a reference to the need to reduce the amount of didactic teaching in British schools. What could this mean?

At first I dismissed it as an unthinking *non sequitur*. After all, the Oxford English Dictionary defines 'didactic' as 'characterised by giving instruction' and 'having the giving of instruction as its aim or object'. Webster is even more specific: 'intended to convey instruction and information as well as pleasure and entertainment'. So surely 'didactic teaching' is tautologous and 'non-didactic teaching' oxymoronic.

But further reflection, particularly on the dictionary definition of 'didactics' as 'systematic instruction', led me to conclude that this apparent confusion was another example of the current lack of consensus about matters educational in Britain today.

For what I suspect lay beneath the call to reduce didactic teaching was not just a semantic slip, but two very different views about the purposes and content of education; about the methods to be used in schools and classrooms; and about the values which underpin the whole process of education.

One view owes much to Rousseau and to Dewey. It emphasises the individual pupil rather than the teacher. It talks of projects and discovery methods, the democratisation of education, the minimising or even the abolition of assessment and examinations. Spontaneity and creativity are the watchwords. Authority of any kind is scarcely mentioned. Formal structures and methods – class teaching, timetables, any rote learning, set and marked work and sometimes even classrooms and subjects – are to be reduced to the bare minimum. For the deschoolers, they are to vanish altogether. The line of separation between teacher and taught is blurred, sometimes to vanishing point. And so the idea of teachers transmitting bodies of knowledge and skills is downgraded – sometimes explicitly and always implicitly.

This view elevates individual self-expression as its guiding principle. The aim of education is to remove the constraints which restrict the growth of the free, spontaneous and autonomous individual. For left to themselves individuals will develop naturally and so acquire the knowledge and skills they need.

It is those holding this view who would be most likely to want to reduce didactic teaching. But attractive though this vision is, the questions it raises are many and deep. To mention but two, how likely is it that individuals will learn very much when most constraints are removed? Is it not more likely that discipline will slacken, with the result that the freedom of pupils who do want to learn may be drastically reduced? And perhaps more important, even if they do want to learn something, who is to provide the knowledge and where is it to be found?

Policies of these kinds, despite the claims made by their advocates, frequently inhibit creativity and diminish freedom. True creativity only flourishes in the tension between spontaneity and disciplined rigorous study. The old saying that genius is 99 parts perspiration and one part inspiration applies to all kinds and levels of learning. And real freedom to learn involves being given a systematic and coherent introduction to well-established skills and bodies of knowledge – or, in other words, being given the 'systematic instruction' which is synonymous with traditional 'didactics'.

Such systematic instruction is also needed in pursuing the two other major purposes of education – the transmission of the traditional culture and moral values which are essential for the survival of any society. But these purposes too are downgraded, either implicitly or explicitly, by the practices of those who urge us in the direction of 'non-didactic teaching'.

These two views of education are not, except in a few schools or individuals, totally distinct and separate. But in most institutions one or other will prevail most or much of the time.

I believe that schools favouring systematic instruction would be in an overwhelming majority amongst independent schools, but would be, relatively speaking, much less common amongst state schools. I also believe that they would feature strongly amongst state schools that are oversubscribed by parents and that research has shown have the kind of ethos which fosters high levels of attainment.

And I suspect that a substantial majority of parents would favour emphasising systematic instruction in knowledge, skills and cultural traditions and values; that teachers would be more evenly divided; while for advisers and educationists the reverse would be true, with the balance coming firmly down on the side of 'non-didactic teaching'.

There would, I suggest, be one significant exception to this rule – in that teachers and educationists would be much more likely to opt for systematic instruction when it is their own children who are involved. This I believe to be the acid test. And, perhaps unsurprisingly, it was one that Rousseau himself never faced. For he brought up none of his own five children. Fearing that they would disturb his creative writings, he abandoned them all to be brought up by a foundling hospital.

So perhaps it should be compulsory for all those professionally involved in education – teachers, heads, school governors, academics, teacher trainers, local advisers, HMI, councillors, MPs, LEA and DES officials, and, last but not least, education correspondents and writers on education – to reveal publicly where their own children were educated. I will start the ball rolling by admitting that my own three children have 18 pupil-years of service in a state primary school, 19 in a state comprehensive school and two in an independent school.

And, even more important, perhaps we should recognise that, given the differences I have outlined, there is no respectable case for persisting with any kind of monolithic or near-monopoly system of education. Instead, we should develop a system of education in which, to put it crudely, we are all able to choose between schools which set out either to teach or not to teach our children. In a democracy there is no other morally acceptable alternative.

This potential dichotomy about what should or should not happen in the classroom is so important for the future of education that it deserves further discussion.

STANDARDS, SUBJECTS AND THE LACK OF CONSENSUS ABOUT EDUCATION

Since the mid-1960s widely differing views have emerged on the nature of education, on teaching and on the prime purpose of schools.

In any assessment of standards reached in individual subjects, it is important to realise that the nature of what is understood by these subjects has been affected, sometimes very radically, by the conflict between those who believe that education is primarily a transmission of knowledge and culture from one generation to the next, and those who think that the individual pupil is the prime mover with a rate of learning mainly determined by his or her individual development, and that teachers should predominantly be helping their pupils to discover the world for themselves, acting as facilitators rather than initiators of the educational process.[2]

This conflict is reflected in different methods of classroom organisation. The dominant method is teacher-centred whole-class instruction for the transmission model, and pupil-centred individual or group situations for the developmental approach. The consequences of these differences have been graphically described by Melanie Phillips in her book *All Must Have Prizes*,[3] in which she rightly characterises the developmental approach as a retreat from teaching.

These conflicts make the assessment of standards of education much more difficult, because some of those who advocate a revised – as opposed to the traditional – interpretation of many subjects also have very different ideas as to what it means to measure 'standards' or to teach traditional subjects, or even to teach in the traditional sense at all, even though they continue to use the traditional subject names and to talk of standards. It is these kinds of views which stimulate that hostility to knowledge and its acquisition, and the related hostility to testing whether or not that knowledge has been successfully acquired by pupils, which is such a puzzle to the layman or to those who have been out of touch with the world of education for a number of years.

This is why nearly every subject on the curriculum is now a battleground. In the next section we will briefly discuss the main traditional subjects one by one.

ENGLISH

The teaching of English in the traditional sense is now frequently not only abandoned but actively deprecated. Teaching of grammar, punctuation or spelling is strongly discouraged, as are attempts to correct pupils' writing or speech. It is even sometimes suggested that any language, dialect or form of speech is as good as any other for any purpose.[4]

Such an approach clearly implies substantial hostility to written examinations and underpins the desire for public assessment of standards in English to be made solely by coursework marked by pupils' own teachers. It also underpins the drift towards open-book public examinations and the circulation of pre-release materials, containing information about the questions to be asked, some weeks before examinations.

In English literature, this 'philosophy' suggests, or sometimes requires, that any text is as good or as valid as any other. It follows that any emphasis on a traditional canon of literature, to which all pupils are entitled to be introduced, is strongly discouraged and deprecated.[5]

MATHEMATICS

In mathematics, there have been strong moves away from traditional methods of teaching, including the learning of tables and the development of skills in mental arithmetic.[6] In English schools, electronic calculators have been readily available from the early primary years onwards. Emphasis has been placed on pupils' own efforts to create what is sometimes referred to as 'their mathematics', and to the setting of tasks for pupils in which they investigate the mathematical world for themselves as a major means by which they learn and are assessed.

The result, if not the intention, has been the loss of the idea that mathematical relationships are exact; very little emphasis on the concept of proof which underpins nearly all serious mathematics; and virtually no emphasis on developing the skills needed for the correct manipulation of either numbers or symbols.

Tests or examinations have been more durable in mathematics than in English, but pupils' performance is now frequently facilitated by the availability in tests and examinations of calculators of all kinds and even by the provision of substantial lists of formulae, including many of the most elementary kind.[7]

SCIENCE

In science, similar trends have been apparent. There has been a conscious aversion, both in the National Curriculum and in many schools, to teaching or even naming the separate and significantly different sciences of physics, chemistry and biology.

Instead of the separate sciences, there has been an emphasis on 'general science' courses in which the content is frequently learnt and assessed by means of 'scientific investigations' conducted by the pupils themselves, even sometimes by the very youngest. These 'investigations' are not experiments set up for illustrative purposes, but are meant to simulate the sort of scientific methods used by researchers. They have proved to be extremely time-consuming and unproductive as pupils sought to emulate trained researchers, or even to re-discover for themselves a tiny part of what had been discovered by so many outstanding individuals over the centuries.

One result has been the stripping from the teaching of physics and chemistry much of the content which requires any demanding mathematics and, sometimes, an emphasis on discussing in 'science' courses the social or environmental aspects of science without pupils knowing anything important about the sciences themselves.

This latter trend is now threatening to dominate the new GCSE science courses that started in 2006 such as Twenty-First Century Science, in which discussions on topics like environmental pollution or climate change often precede the acquisition of the basic knowledge needed to discuss these topics with any hope of achieving an informed opinion or reaching valid conclusions.

HISTORY

In history, the 'new history' has down-played the knowledge of facts or of chronology and has also explicitly reduced the importance of political history. The focus has changed to the cultivation of empathy with those who lived in the past and to the evaluation of historical source materials, but *without* giving pupils the background knowledge needed to empathise or to make such evaluations with any hope of validity. It is, once again, as if the methods of the historical researcher were being transplanted into schools, even into primary schools.

One near-casualty of these trends has been the historical essay, which is now seldom required and which pupils frequently have neither the command of English nor the historical knowledge to undertake.

FRENCH AND OTHER MODERN FOREIGN LANGUAGES

The tendencies discussed for English also apply to French and other modern foreign languages. The teaching of grammar, and its correction, is not now emphasised. Another near-casualty has been the skill of translation from English into French (or any other language). The 'authentic' way of learning French is to speak it and to acquire it as a native Frenchman would do, but, of course, pupils cannot have the total immersion in the language over many years and from an early age that native Frenchmen themselves experience. Assessing standards has also been substantially changed, with the use of dictionaries in examinations now commonplace.

CONCLUSION

The various tendencies discussed for each of the traditional subjects can be seen to have a number of factors in common – a hostility to knowledge, a belief in the capacity of pupils to learn or even to discover things, however complex, for themselves, and the substantial down-playing of both testing and examinations and even of teaching itself in the traditional sense of that term. Much of what has been advocated over many years by educationists – and which is now accepted by thousands of teachers up and down the country – amounts to a retreat from teaching, but not one that has been accepted by most parents of the children affected.

These changes in what many educators mean by education are an important part of the context which needs to be borne in mind in the rest of this chapter.

WHAT THIS HAS MEANT FOR PARENTS – SUMMARY OF NATIONAL STANDARDS

Low average standards

Overall standards are low; the average standard achieved by pupils at 11 and 14 is significantly below the standard they should reach for their ages.

The shortfall between actual standards and expected standards increases for older pupils. At the age of seven they are, on average, a little ahead of expected standards, but by 11 they are about a year behind and by 14 two years behind.

Enormous variations between schools

The spread between the standards of different schools of the same type is very large indeed. It increases from about 2.5 years at age seven (the range of 'subject ages' is from about six to 8.5 years), to nearly four years at age 11 (from about 8.25 to 11.75 years), to five years or more at age 14 (from about nine or less to 14 or more years).

These enormous differences between schools are very important for parents because they mean that the school they go to can make a comparably enormous difference to the standards achieved by their children.

These differences between schools are particularly important in primary schools, where a secure knowledge of reading and arithmetic in particular are crucial for much learning at later stages. We will therefore give some specific examples of what these variations may mean for individual pupils.

READING AND ARITHMETIC

Standards achieved by individual pupils in arithmetic[8]

What these enormous differences in standards between individual schools mean for individual pupils can be illustrated by results for individual arithmetic questions in an Ofsted study of standards in mathematics.[9]

At seven years old two of the questions asked were:
– addition of a two-digit number and a single-digit number without carrying (written question);
– multiplication of two single-digit numbers (mental arithmetic)

At 11 years old two of the questions asked were:
– addition of two simple fractions (written question)
– state two numbers with a given difference (mental arithmetic)

For each of these four questions about 40 per cent of pupils overall gave the right answer, but *the figures for individual schools varied from about 5 per cent to about 90 per cent of pupils.* Such enormous differences are even more alarming since the actual questions are very easy indeed:

Seven-year-olds
(50 + 5)
(2 × 5)

11-year-olds
(1/2 + 1/4)
write two numbers which differ by 11.

It would be difficult to imagine easier examples of the specific types of questions than these. Nevertheless, in some schools the overwhelming majority of pupils got them wrong.

Standards achieved by individual pupils in reading

Low standards in reading for individual pupils in three LEAs are described in another Ofsted study.[10]

> **Seven-year-olds**
> The 7-year-old test results showed that only 1 in 5 pupils achieved a reading age at or above their chronological age ... 79% were below average and almost 1 in 5 pupils achieved no score at all (after two years at school).
>
> **11-year-olds**
> ... 2 in 5 achieved a reading age at or above their chronological age. About 1 in 3 pupils had reading ages two to four years below their chronological age. White pupils from economically disadvantaged backgrounds consistently performed least well and constituted the largest group of under-achievers ...

Ofsted concluded:

> The wide gulf in pupils' reading performance is serious and unacceptable. Some schools and pupils are doing well against the odds while others in similar circumstances are not. It is clear that it is what individual schools do that makes the difference to their pupils' reading performance.

For both seven- and 11-year-olds Ofsted identified poor and insufficient teaching of phonic skills as a major cause of underachievement. Ofsted also said that: 'Underachievement in reading is a major threat to pupils' educational progress in both primary and secondary education.'

That was in 1996, but even then the problem of low and variable standards of reading was not new. In a paper called

Sponsored Reading Failure, published in 1991, the author Martin Turner wrote that:

> Literacy, the point of access to the entire cultural heritage, falls to the responsibility of the teachers of the youngest children.

Turner is one of the educational psychologists who, in June 1991, drew attention to the apparent fall in reading standards amongst seven- and eight-year-olds in eight LEAs. The average reported decline for 1985–89 was substantial – over three points of standard score implying a 50 per cent rise in the proportion of very poor readers. The decline showed up over a range of tests; the number of pupils tested over the five years was more than a quarter of a million – equivalent each year to nearly 10 per cent of all the seven-year-olds in the country.

Such a fall is important. Reading failure at seven frequently means continuing problems throughout school and beyond. It can cut children off from their culture and history as well as denying them basic skills, like reading warning notices or filling in forms.

A prime factor in the perceived decline, according to Turner, is the 'real books' movement for learning to read which downplays the direct teaching of alphabetic reading. Phonic methods, stressing the learning of the sounds of individual letters, are decried as merely instilling 'decoding skills' despite research over more than two decades showing such methods to be most effective in teaching reading. The result of these 'real books' methods can be 'numerous children, demotivated for life not only from books real and unreal but from school altogether', and thus requiring 'expensive and very directive remedial education'.

But one thing is perhaps even more shocking than the facts – that they had to be brought to light in a clandestine fashion. The LEAs involved were not named and, to protect the psychologists, the full test details were suppressed.

At the time, officials frequently prevented such data from becoming known, while in many LEAs the collection of test data was discouraged or discontinued. Nor at the time was there any national monitoring of reading standards.

Nowhere in education is open public discussion more important than in the teaching and assessment of the basic skill of reading. As Turner put it: 'What, on a commonsense view, could possibly be political about teaching young children to read?' So it ought to be simple to get all concerned to agree that if we really want children to read, we do have to teach them. And it ought to be simple to establish that, whatever else is jettisoned from the National Curriculum testing programme at seven, reading is one skill which must be taught and tested effectively.

As simple as ABC, one might say, if that time-honoured phrase had not gone out of fashion precisely because the accepted 'wisdom' in the educational world has swung against teaching children to read in the traditional way.

THE NATIONAL LITERACY STRATEGY

Martin Turner's work and the Ofsted reports cited above, published when Chris Woodhead was Chief Inspector of Schools, led the Government – first the Conservatives under John Major and then New Labour under Tony Blair – to try to develop a National Literacy Strategy for all primary schools.

But this fell foul of battles between the advocates of the status quo – primarily the whole language or 'real books' methods which, together with the still fashionable disorderly classrooms described above, were then in the ascendant – and the advocates of teaching phonics first and fast. The result was a mish-mash – called 'mixed methods' – which satisfied nobody and, more important, did little or nothing to raise standards.

So after a decade of further – and unnecessary – reading failure an inquiry was set up in June 2005 under the chairmanship of Jim Rose, an experienced inspector who had served as one of Chris Woodhead's deputies in charge of primary schools, following an influential report *Teaching Children to Read* in April 2005, by the House of Commons Select Committee on Education. And this time the Rose Report, *Independent review of the teaching of early reading*, in March 2006, was unequivocal, as was a similar report *Teaching Reading: National Inquiry into the Teaching of Literacy* in December 2005, in Australia. This is how it was described by John Clare in the *Daily Telegraph*:

> The reading report, by Jim Rose, a former chief inspector of primary schools, strongly criticised teachers for leaving children to 'ferret out on their own how the alphabetic code works'. It effectively called for the Government's literacy strategy to be torn up.
>
> It said the fundamental principle of the strategy – that children should be taught by a variety of methods, including guessing at words according to their context and memorising them by their shape – should be replaced by the traditional method known as 'phonics first and fast'.
>
> Mr Rose said that this approach offered the vast majority of beginners the best route to becoming skilled readers. At present, about one in three children do not, mostly because the mixture of methods they are subjected to 'can amount to a daunting and confusing experience'.
>
> The report, which was accepted without reservation by Ruth Kelly, the Education Secretary, emphasised that teachers were 'more than capable of meeting the professional demands of teaching phonic work well'.
>
> It suggested that they had failed to do so because, as a profession, they had come to believe that phonics teaching would discourage 'a love of good books and positive attitudes to reading', a view Mr Rose strongly rejected.
>
> 'Ensuring that children master the alphabetic code is at the heart of phonic work', the report said. 'However, daily systematic phonics teaching does not mean that children are not exposed to the wealth of good literature and favourite books.'
>
> ... for Miss Kelly, the light dawned this year with the publication of a seven-year study in Clackmannanshire

> that demonstrated beyond all doubt that children taught phonics first and fast outperformed their peers who had been subjected to the National Literacy Strategy's approach.[11]

There is therefore now strong evidence regarding how important the early and systematic teaching of synthetic phonics is for standards of reading, and, more important, there is a clear public commitment to ensuring that primary schools implement these recommendations.

And there is also evidence – both systematic and anecdotal – that many pupils have been categorised as having special educational needs when they have not been given systematic structured teaching of reading in their early months and years in school.

As the changes recommended by Jim Rose gradually take effect, we could therefore also see a considerable reduction, year on year, in the number of pupils deemed to have special educational needs.[12]

It is surely a fundamental human right in the modern world to be taught to read. And it is a national scandal, amounting to child abuse on a substantial scale, that so many children have been deprived of that right for so long; but, at last, we may be on the verge of doing something effective about it.

However, there is much less agreement about the effective teaching of arithmetic.

WHAT CAN AND SHOULD BE DONE ABOUT THE TEACHING OF ARITHMETIC

What can and should be done follows directly from the arguments and discussion given in a pamphlet I wrote over a decade ago.[13]

First, the National Curriculum should be brought into line with national curricula in other countries by putting much more emphasis on arithmetic in Key Stages 1 & 2, cutting out the separate sections on Data Handling and Using and Applying Mathematics, and ceasing to require the use of calculators in primary schools. Moreover, all National Curriculum tests should be done without the use of calculators. This could and should be done at once. It is ridiculous that we should continue to require teachers to follow by law practices which are detrimental to the sound learning of the foundations of mathematics, particularly when all that is required is a change in Statutory Regulations, which can be passed very quickly given all-party agreement, rather than primary legislation.

Second, the National Curriculum Tests in Mathematics at ages seven and 11 should focus primarily on accuracy in basic arithmetic, both mental and written. Such tests should be produced in standardised form so as to give as much discrimination and accurate information as possible, and their results should be published forthwith, school by school. Once again, this should be done at once, even if it means changing the vague and imprecise eight-level National Curriculum scale.

Third, it will be necessary to bring about significant changes in teaching styles, classroom organisation and the use of simple teaching aids such as blackboards and textbooks along the lines which have proved to be so successful in other countries. The motivation for such changes should be sought in greater knowledge of what can be achieved – perhaps by the use of videos and exchange visits.[14] It would also be helpful if more use could be made of what has been learnt about adopting continental teaching practices in English schools in a continuing project in the London Borough of Barking and Dagenham.[15] Let us, for a change, try to make 'good primary practice' mean what it says.

Finally, particular efforts will need to be made to produce much better textbooks and Teachers' Guides, perhaps by experimenting with translating existing continental books or using the official textbooks from Singapore, which scores very highly in international studies of standards in mathematics and still uses English as the language of instruction in its schools and hence in its textbooks.[16]

THE IMPORTANCE OF ARITHMETIC

In conclusion, let us remind ourselves why the proper teaching of basic arithmetic is so important.

It is important because, if learnt at the right early age, it provides the key to a whole host of practical applications in all walks of life.

And it is even more important because the precision of arithmetic, if properly taught, performs two vital intellectual functions. It provides a model for the later introduction of algebra, itself a kind of generalised arithmetic, which is one of the glories of the development of mathematics in the work of Viete and Descartes in the 16th and 17th centuries, and which later provided the basis of the differential and integral calculus.[17] And it provides a first taste of, and schooling in, a discipline in which the results are absolutely exact and precise. Such an understanding is vital to the later appreciation of the importance of exact proof in mathematics or in logic. As one experienced teacher of mathematics has put it:

> In mathematics, the '=' symbol conveys a *moral* message ... once the moral imperative of the '=' symbol is lost, mathematics becomes no more than an experimentally based bag of tricks.[18]

So let us have the courage to call it 'arithmetic' and to teach it in ways which will lay the right foundations for the later stages of education and provide a proper logical, and practical, foundation for the minds of the next generation.[19]

CONCLUSION

The remedies described above for some of the ills outlined in the first part of this chapter only apply to the very earliest stages of education. Much more will be needed if the current malaise afflicting the education of our future citizens is to be corrected. But what is proposed here could well have a knock-on effect on what comes later and would at least mean that our children were being given the start they need.

APPENDIX

The teachers' plot to make our children into failures

by Minette Marrin

The *Daily Telegraph*, 17 December 1998

There is an incentive for schools to register children as having special educational needs. It provides an advance excuse for bad results.

If the price of freedom is eternal vigilance, the price of vigilance is eternal tedium. There can be very little more tedious than fossicking about in local government papers and sitting through dreary town hall meetings. And few people can be much interested in the day-to-day minutiae of education policy and the running of schools. But it is the minutiae that matter.

Take special educational needs, for instance. How the heart sinks; the subject falls unmistakably into the category of important but boring, and best left to experts. Yet I wonder whether it is best left to experts, or whether it is being left to real experts. For once, I think that, on closer inspection, there is something sensational about this unappealing subject. What is going on in this field seems, from a common sense view, both astonishing and shocking.

What proportion of primary school children would you expect to have special educational needs, as reasonably understood? I mean children who, for some special reason, cannot cope with ordinary classes in the ordinary way, and find it significantly harder to learn than their peers – children who have specifically educational needs, which ought to be met in some special individual way, unlike those of normal children. Common sense suggests that, across the population, such children would be fairly rare.

For instance, across the population, you would expect to find only 0.33 per cent of children between five and 14 with a mental handicap or intellectual disability, according to figures from the Office of Populations, Censuses and Surveys. Only 2 to 4 per cent of people suffer from dyslexia, as strictly defined, according to the educational psychologist Martin Turner, of the Dyslexia Institute. Less than 0.01 per cent of people suffer from autism. Attention deficit disorder is notoriously difficult to define, but probably does not affect more than 5 per cent of children, if as many. Then there are serious psychological problems, visual handicaps and disabling medical problems. All these disabilities add up, but to what? To what proportion?

It is astonishing to discover that there are many primary schools across the country where 40 per cent of the children are registered by their teachers as having special educational needs. In the London Borough of Tower Hamlets, for instance, there are only six schools that have fewer than 20 per cent of children registered with SEN. Twenty-four schools have more than 20 per cent of children with SEN, 18 schools have 30 per cent or more, seven have well over 40 per cent, and one has 55 per cent. Tower Hamlets is not alone in having these astonishing proportions of SEN children. Britain lists far more than other European countries, as the DfES admits. Clearly, in this country, all too many teachers think that special educational needs are not really special at all, but more or less normal.

One might argue, and people do, that Tower Hamlets has particular problems – poverty, overcrowding and many children who do not speak English as a first language. However, the Government's SEN code of practice specifically says that a child must not be regarded as having a learning difficulty solely because the language of his home is different from the language in which he will be taught.

And there is no reason to suppose that Tower Hamlets children have more disabilities than other children, or that SEN are genuinely so common. Ruth Miskin is the head teacher of the Kobi Nazrul school in Tower Hamlets, and she, apparently, doesn't believe it either. Most untypically, she has registered only five pupils (3 per cent of her school) as having SEN. Yet her children are not selected in any way. They come from exactly the same catchment area as the Tower Hamlets schools that have registered 30 to 40 per cent of their children. There is no special selection.

Nearly 80 per cent of the children at Kobi Nazrul are Bangladeshi; English is their second language, and some arrive at school hardly speaking any. In 1997, 63 per cent of the pupils qualified for free school meals, a clear indication of poverty. The average class size is 27.5. Seventy per cent of the children in the local ward live in overcrowded households, according to the latest census.

Yet these children have consistently done extremely well; they scored above the national average in reading, writing and maths, in the recent government tests (SATs). They scored easily the highest in Tower Hamlets in reading tests and got an excellent inspection report from Ofsted. All the seven-year-olds at Kobi Nazrul, without exception, can read.

Something stands out a mile here: a negligible rate of SEN registration seems to go with a very high rate of reading success. That is because Ruth Miskin and her staff are passionately interested in literacy – she believes that every healthy child can learn to read – and particularly in a rigorous system of phonics, about which she has lectured and written a great deal. Properly taught, a comprehensive phonics system enables children to learn very fast, with great confidence. This means they avoid the common sense of failure and frustration of poor readers, and the disruptive behaviour that goes with it, which also leads to SEN registration.

Effectively, phonics keeps children off the SEN register. On closer inspection, it emerges that an enormous proportion of SEN children, perhaps as large as three-quarters, are labelled that way simply because they cannot read, or cannot learn to read. That is not because something is wrong with them; there's something wrong with the way they're taught. 'Most of what schools see as SEN has to do with illiteracy, and much of it is created by the schools themselves,' says Martin Turner. 'Most literacy teaching is ineffective and children are being crippled as a result.'

The perversity of this is hard to believe, but perverse it is. Above all, there is a perverse incentive to register lots of children as having special educational needs; it provides an excuse in advance for any failure. It must be tempting to attach the failure to the child, rather than to the teacher or the school or the teaching method. The absurdity is that, being registered as having special needs does not mean that the child will get any special attention, other than meetings with parents and SEN co-ordinators.

Very often it is not much more than a label of failure and a list of unambitious targets; real personal help is rarely forthcoming. Government advisers are apparently aware of this, and anxious to keep the Literacy Project on course. Perhaps a good start would be to assume that where a child cannot learn to read, it is probably the teacher who has a special educational need – a problem in teaching reading, a difficulty with understanding the value of phonics and a slowness to understand that almost every child can learn to read, even some of the truly disabled.

CHAPTER 11

COMMUNITY COHESION AND CATHOLIC EDUCATION

ARCHBISHOP VINCENT NICHOLS

Central to much of the policy of the present Government is what is called 'social' or 'community' cohesion, a concern that, as a society, we should progress along the pathway of mutual understanding and harmonious cooperation with each other, no matter our differences. This is an absolutely proper aim for any government.

The discussion about community cohesion in our society has reached a critical point.

In this brief chapter, I would like to highlight what seem to me to be some basic perceptions that are being overlooked or distorted in this discussion.

But first of all, some current indicators of the state of the debate.

The Government's 'Commission on Integration and Cohesion' was established to 'engage in a new and honest debate about integration and cohesion in the UK' (Ruth Kelly, Introductory Statement). This debate 'will have considerably more value if we can be open and honest about the challenges we face ... we must not tiptoe around important issues' (ibid). The remit of the Commission is described as 'considering how local areas can make the most of the benefits delivered by increasing diversity' and 'how they can respond to the tensions it can sometimes cause'.

In its Interim Report, the Commission has highlighted some of the problems of this area of work: how to respect difference without inadvertently promoting separation; how to encourage 'interaction' on the basis of a shared set of values; how to make it clear that cohesion is a challenge to every community; and how to identify common barriers to its promotion. It rejects easy rhetoric about 'multi-culturalism' and 'assimilation'. It asserts: 'integration and cohesion are all about people ... and people from communities, not just minority groups.' It has much work to do.

It is clear that education is one of the keys to these tasks. It is quite reasonable that Catholic schools, and other faith schools, be asked to give an account of how they contribute to mutual understanding and peaceful community living. Indeed, Catholic schools can respond positively to such questions, with examples of schools contributing significantly to their local community and certainly equipping young people with the skills needed for the development of adult and lasting mutual understanding with others in society.

But in saying that education is a key, I do not mean that the social patterns of those who attend a particular school are key. To focus on admissions and on the 'social mix' of a school is to project the problem of community cohesion onto schools, and to make them bear the brunt of its challenge – and indeed bear the brunt of the blame. To me this is short-sighted, unfounded on evidence, and simply a politically convenient shifting of the blame. It is little more than putting the sins of adults onto the shoulders of their children.

Education is, of course, a key to making the most of the God-given talents of every person and preparing them to make a constructive contribution to a modern society. Schooling is about preparation for adult life. It is not the performance. The test of an inclusive society does not lie in that society's schools, but in its adult activity. The real task of education is to prepare youngsters with the mind-set, the skills and the understanding to take their part, as adults, in a profoundly mixed and pressurised society. Schools are not social workshops. They are places of education. They must be judged on their educational achievements, understood, of course, in the widest sense.

The recently published report, 'Quality and Performance: A Survey of Education in Catholic Schools', highlights the achievements of our schools, illustrating in detail how they do indeed prepare pupils for life in modern Britain. It shatters some of the current myths about Catholic education (cf. 'Quality and Performance: A Survey of Education in Catholic Schools', Catholic Education Service, Oct. 2006, available at: general@cesew.co.uk).

The recent paper put before the House of Bishops of the Church of England lamented the fact that in much thinking about community cohesion the role of Christianity and of Church schools is being overlooked. This is true. On the whole, in popular political debate, there is little positive attention paid to the cohesive influence of Church schools up and down this land for the last hundred years at least. A broad Christian ethic is the cement of our society. It is not so frequently expressed as such, but the fact is that notions of compassion for the underdog, respect for the stranger, great charity for those in need, and tolerance of the eccentric or the unusual, are all based on the fundamental message of the Christian Gospel. Removed from these roots, it is highly unlikely that these crucial values will survive. The Christian Churches, with their schools, are crucial to social cohesion in the vast majority of communities in this country.

But I want to look more deeply at two particular themes of cohesion, particularly from a Catholic point of view. These two themes were well expressed in the address of Pope Benedict XVI at Regensburg University on 12 September 2006. That speech attracted enormous publicity. But its main challenge was not so much to Islam but to our society, our western liberal democracy. That, of course, was neatly deflected by a media that does not wish to have its key assumptions challenged.

His challenge was well expressed in one sentence:

> A reason which is deaf to the divine and which relegates religion into the realm of subcultures is incapable of entering into the dialogue of cultures.

This, it seems to me, describes so accurately much of our current debate. On the one hand, as a society, we recognise only too well that we have to bring together people for whom religious faith is significant, if not central, to their most profound thoughts about themselves and their lives. This is true for the 72 per cent of people in this country who described themselves as Christian. It is true for the small but significant number of Muslims who now are at home in this country. It is true for the Jewish, Sikh, Hindu and Buddhist communities; it is true for people from India, and for Poles and many others who are coming here from EU nations. This is the fact. Yet our politicians seem to live in a different world, a world that is purely secular and material, a world that does not permit a mature consideration of the key role of religious belief. We even have those who suggest that part of the way to prepare youngsters to live in this society is by making it easy for them to opt out of religious worship, and even religious education, while at school. Behind this, at the end of the day, is the assertion that religious influences are bad for you, and that ignorance of religion is better than exposure to it and the study of it.

Why is this so? Pope Benedict points very clearly to the roots of this misunderstanding and prejudice against religious belief. It lies in the distorted and truncated notion of reason which shapes our society and, to a large extent, the education it offers.

Quite simply we have sold our soul to a positivistic understanding of reason. By this is meant that knowledge and reasoning are limited to what can be positively seen, measured and physically tested through hypothesis, experiment and observation. As the French philosopher Auguste Comte, one of the fathers of positivism and the first to coin the word 'sociology', wrote in the 1850s:

> All sound thinkers since Bacon hold that the only authentic knowledge is that based on observable facts.

Everything else becomes a matter of personal judgement or opinion. Here I have expressed very crudely a complex issue. In doing so I do not want to appear to be dismissive of positivist science or reasoning. As Pope Benedict said:

> The positive aspects of modernity are to be acknowledged unreservedly: we are all grateful for the marvellous possibilities that it has opened up for mankind and for the progress in humanity that has been granted to us. The scientific ethos, moreover, is the will to be obedient to the truth, and as such it embodies an attitude which reflects one of the basic tenets of Christianity.

But positivist knowledge and reasoning contain their own limitation. They strive for a genuine scientific objectivity. The observer, the scientist, must strive to remove as far as possible subjective interpretation or manipulation of the 'facts'. While this objectivity gives positivist reasoning a kind of universality, an independence from sentiment, race, nation, class etc, it is normative only on the basis of what has been observed, measured and taken to its logical conclusion.

What positive knowledge and reasoning cannot do is provide anything that is normative in value or moral judgement. They can discover, magnificently, what can be done. They cannot, properly, provide an answer to the question, 'But should it be done?' Positivist thinking is quite different from moral thinking, for moral values are not capable of being subjected to the rigour of positivist enquiry. But nor is positivist reasoning capable of producing moral thought or principle. And this is the very heart of our problem.

Moral reasoning, on the other hand, can start with the experienced reality of the person and become a 'trans-subjective' way of thinking, and thereby construct a moral framework which has an objectivity of its own. So, for example, the experience of truth and goodness moves the thinking person beyond themselves into another kind of reasoning, and one which opens up whole new frontiers. Moral reasoning overcomes the 'singularity' of self, or the 'individualism' of a positivist culture. Moral reasoning provides a solid basis for moral community in a way which positivist reasoning cannot.

And that is crucial to the task of generating a shared mind and spirit between people.

A society which, consciously or unconsciously, limits itself – and its education – to a positivist understanding of reason will find itself unable to determine shared moral principles and values. Such a society will lack cohesion. More importantly, it will be denying itself precisely the means of producing a degree of moral cohesion which is essential for shared projects and ambitions for social living. Yet those means are in fact available within our capacity of reasoning, properly understood.

In practice, moral reasoning can begin with reflection on every situation in which truth and goodness are experienced. Then moral reflection takes place, seeking to understand what is meant by the truth and the good, how it is to be explored and defined. Clearly the first place is the family and the setting in which a child first grows. Then, every friendship and interpersonal relationship has its contribution to make, for good or bad.

Yet the school has a crucial role to play in such reflection and in the development of moral reasoning. Every school should be able to give a reasoned account of its moral perspectives. It should be able to put forward its vision of 'moral communion'. This is essential to the capacity of the school to contribute to education. After all, education is incomplete without drawing its participants into this proper and crucial joint project: the school as a moral community. Only then does a school become a place in which students are properly prepared for the contribution they shall make to our society and its cohesiveness.

A school which cannot do this is not able to make its proper contribution to genuine community cohesion. It is rather futile to demand that schools teach 'citizenship' if there is neither agreement over the moral values that contribute to that citizenship, nor acceptance of the use of reason to lead us to universal values which form the basis of our common good. Appeals to 'neutrality' in education are empty. It is simply not possible to offer 'value-free education'. When that is claimed, all that happens is that the values which inform the education become covert. Today some appeal to human rights as a way of filling this void. But human rights, whether expressed in a Universal Charter or by an NHS Charter of Patients' Rights, are only part of the story. It is the moral reasoning behind such rights that is crucial, not least because that reasoning leads to an appreciation of corresponding duties.

This is clearly evidenced in some aspects of the Sexual Orientation Regulations recently put in place. These Regulations have asserted the rights of same-sex partnerships over the rights of the exercise of the religious belief of the Christian Churches and most other faiths within the public services of adoption. This has been done without any reasoned debate about the parenting needs of children, not in individual hard cases, but in principle. These needs should have been central to this discussion, yet they have hardly figured at all. An appeal to rights, and to adult rights, has been given precedence. Yet such an appeal does not constitute, by itself, a reasoned moral discourse.

Indeed, there is a complex debate to be held about the nature and application of human rights, within which there is quite a conflict between a constitutional understanding of human rights and an ethical understanding. We need far more discussion about the connection between moral principles and the morality of behaviour, on the one hand, and the language and use of human rights on the other (cf. J. Rivers, 'The Church in the Age of Human Rights' in *International Journal for the Study of the Christian Church*, Vol. 7, No. 1, 2007).

Catholic education is well placed to engage in such moral discourse. Its understanding of reason is not truncated. Its 'moral communion' is well spelt out. It is, indeed, a major factor in what is described, and esteemed, as the ethos of Catholic schools.

But the kind of moral reasoning we need contradicts the fundamental liberal, secular claim that the crucial characteristic of the human being is that each is an individual. Within the perspectives of this claim, all that limits individuality is to be resisted. Indeed, society itself is no more than a construct which allows individuals to exist and flourish without becoming enemies to one another. Moral reasoning, on the other hand, explores the truth that every human being is, essentially, communitarian, coming into being only in a complex of relationships and finding fulfilment only within relationships. Shared moral reasoning as a basis for community cohesion is the alternative to radical individualism which has led us, so far, on a path that is clearly divisive and inimical to a cohesive society.

But the argument about the place of reason in our Western society goes further.

Moral reasoning takes seriously human interiority. It seeks to hold together the physical, emotional and spiritual reality of the person, with its focus on the moral question: 'What is a good life?' Such reasoning leads us inevitably into the arena of religious belief.

The relationship between the spiritual and the religious is one of the crucial questions of today. It is being explored, and exploited, in the Health Service and, to some extent, in the Prison Service, too. In those arenas the 'religious' is being collapsed into the generically 'spiritual'. But that will not do.

Any reflection on the spiritual experience of the person, and certainly the person in community, can see how that inner, spiritual life of itself reaches out for wider expression. And any examination of the sweep of mankind's spiritual experience shows how that spiritual quest is met by a gift from without. In Christianity, that gift is known to be the revelation of God in Christ.

What is crucial, of course, is to understand the relationship between that spiritual quest of the reasoning, moral person and the transcendent gift of revelation. In Christian understanding the two meet. In Catholic understanding they do no violence to each other. Faith, the response to revelation, fulfils our human capacity and destiny. Revelation makes clear the true potential of our nature and of our reasoning. Faith complements reason, and illuminates exactly the capabilities of that reasoning. Faith and reason are the two wings on which the human spirit soars.

The implications of this are, of course, considerable.

In the first place, it makes clear why a society which has limited its appreciation of reasoning to its positivist uses will have little comprehension of the true role of religious faith. Such a society will cast faith as irrational and unscientific and therefore not admissible to the public forum or, indeed, to the forum of the university. Such a society will tolerate what it disdainfully calls 'a faith-based education' as if there was something demeaning to education in its association with faith. And it will quickly seize any opportunity to limit or suppress such education. It will do so without regard for the contribution that education inspired by faith actually makes to the well-being of society. It will act out of prejudice.

More positively, this understanding of the role of reason in faith will provide a strong basis for cooperation between those who genuinely seek the well-being of society on the basis of all that reason can offer. Here is solid ground for dialogue between faith communities and government on the whole range of vexing issues that face our society. I willingly admit that in many cases this is precisely what takes place.

Similarly, the recognition of the role of reason in faith and the contribution of faith to reason is an important impetus for dialogue between the major faiths. This, clearly, was part of the invitation of Pope Benedict in his Regensburg lecture, even to the detail of choosing the quotation from the 13th-century dialogue of the Emperor Manuel II. The point under discussion was that of the use of violence in spreading the faith. The Emperor asserted that to do so was against the nature of God because it was unreasonable. The Emperor said: 'God is not pleased by blood, and not acting reasonably is contrary to God's nature.' This level of interfaith dialogue, involving the place of reason in our exploration of the mystery of God, is something to which we must return, not least in order to strengthen the capacity of the faiths to speak together to government about the well-being of our society.

Finally, this understanding of faith and reason together lifting us to our true capacity, both as individuals and as a society, must have its impact on our conduct of religious education. It is clear that the strengthening and maturing of faith, which we seek, requires a deepening appreciation of the role of faith in completing and fulfilling our human nature and, in particular, its harmony with true reasoning. But this is no easy task, especially as for so long religious belief has retreated from the onslaught of positivist thinking into the enclave of personal conviction, or has taken the route of unreasoning fundamentalism. If we are to play our full part in the task of building our new society, then we need to show quite clearly the strength of our faith in terms that are accessible to others. This can only be achieved in two ways: in the recovery of the true capacity of reasoning for both moral and religious insight; and, of course, in the witness of lives well lived, the evidence of schools well run.

How ironic it is that in our public culture a cynicism about religious faith has taken hold. Have we, quite simply, lost our nerve when it comes to the reality of religious belief? We have lost our nerve because, as a society, we have taken the road of relegating all these matters to the sphere of the private and of seeking to build our society, our cohesiveness on the secular/material instead. Yet there will never be a truly cohesive society that does not take seriously the spiritual quest of its people, in all the forms of that quest, and which does not give a space in its public culture for the religious beliefs of its people. The rigorously secular, liberal project of community cohesion is mistaken in its fundamental view of the human person and simply will not work.

There may well be now a growing awareness of this. At present, alongside a public discourse that belittles faith schools and the contribution they can make, there is no doubt about the popularity of Catholic and other faith schools among so many people. Is this why those who espouse the secular liberal view of society speak out so vehemently against faith schools, not simply because they are opposed to religious faith, but because all that a faith-centred education stands for exposes the fallacies of their position? While one driving force for community cohesion is, for some, the need to eliminate difference, or at least control of the impact of differences, for others the true richness of life lies in appreciating and critically evaluating, by reasoned discourse, the values held in these differences and working together in mutually respectful cooperation on shared projects.

Properly understood and carried out, Catholic education serves community cohesion. Catholic education seeks to provide its pupils with the patterns of moral reasoning by which mature free choice can be exercised in the pursuit of lasting happiness. Catholic education seeks precisely to hand on, in a process of continual understanding and exploration, the values that are fundamental to human well-being, sustained and enabled by a relationship to the Creator. Catholic education equips its students to enter into a plural society with wisdom and discernment, with principles and virtues, rather than with the purely political values of tolerance and the suspension of personal judgement. Catholic education helps its pupils to understand themselves correctly as members of a community, as nurtured and sustained by a community and as contributing to that community. Catholic education explores the proper relationship between the individual and society, not the distorted model of our public culture. Catholic education helps its pupils to give an account of the faith that forms them, to speak of it with confidence, and to know that, through it, they can meet with members of other faiths with sensitivity and insight. Catholic education does not encourage its students to approach religious faith at arm's length, as if it is something of which to be only suspicious, for such suspicion quickly corrodes the mutual understanding and esteem that true community cohesion actually requires.

Of course, while having these aims, Catholic education does not always succeed. But what is clear is that over the last hundred years the project of Catholic education in this country has gone from strength to strength, from a position of being on the margins of society to one in which it makes an acknowledged and appreciated contribution to the common good. That experience of exclusion is important for us to remember. Others in our society, in their turn, are now experiencing it, are being the subject of suspicion. We must surely have encouraging words for them, encouraging them into partnerships with public authorities, and exploring with them the difficulties of achieving the level of mutual understanding that makes such partnerships effective. We must say to them that the effort is worth it, that the struggle is valid, and that the contribution that they, too, will be able to make will one day be appreciated as long as their effort is ultimately and clearly for the common good of all.

A key issue in current political debate, and one that faces each political party, is to reach clarity about the way in which religious faith and public life relate to each other. Those who wish to rid our public and political life of all evidence of or reference to religious belief represent one extreme. But the way forward is surely for us to be exploring how religious belief, which is such a powerful motivator of 'social generosity', is brought into an intelligent relationship with public structures which correctly seek to be secular. But 'secular' does not mean 'anti-religious'. It means recognising the proper spheres of religious belief and practice on the one hand, and, on the other, the structures of democratic government which are open and accountable to all, with their own criteria of action and their own limitations.

In putting forward the importance of Citizenship Education, OFSTED, in its report of September 2006, stated clearly that citizenship is concerned with taking forward the notion of 'critical democracy'. This, of course, raises the key question of the basis on which this critique is formed. It must be, essentially, a moral critique and requires foundations, principles and lived experience in community. The faiths present in our society represent all of those features and have a major and positive contribution to make to the work of community cohesion.

CHAPTER 12

SEEKING GOD: REFLECTIONS ON A HIDDEN TRADITION

ABBOT AIDAN BELLENGER

The Catholic Church in England, we are now told, is the most numerous 'Faith' community in our country. The national religious profile is in the process of being transformed. With the parallel rise of the Islamic population, religion is becoming again a crucial element in contemporary life and politics. We may not like it, but fundamentalism is again an issue. This disturbs the complacency and inherent intolerance of what has become the new secular, liberal establishment. Have we not reached 'the end of history' and is not Christianity (and especially Catholicism) an anachronistic superstition? Change, change, change ... Aren't things bad enough already?

There is a strongly 'anti-religious' feel to much of the contemporary academe and media. Even if religion is, as Timothy Radcliffe defines it, 'the ultimate goal and purpose of our lives', contemporary thinkers generally ignore it. Natural scientists, especially biologists and, spectacularly, Richard Dawkins, see religion as an irrelevance and attack it with almost evangelical fervour as a barrier to a proper 'scientific' study of the world. Philosophy has grown beyond the once central question of God's existence, and modernists and postmodernists alike look nonplussed at religious questions. Only historians seem to be aware of the importance of religion in political and cultural life, and religion clearly defined, not as part of the mush of multiculturalism.

My perspective on these questions comes from my life as a Benedictine monk living in a country monastery seemingly far (at least superficially) from the city. This makes me, I suppose, a marginal man, but it is one of the insights of the present age that the margins can be the most exciting and creative places. I am also a historian, and I have specialised in two very contrasting periods of European history: the Middle Ages, the so-called 'Age of Faith'; and the French Revolution, stemming from the 'Age of Reason', which put into doubt all traditional institutions. What follows reflects my double identity.

'Secular society' is an ideal which stems from the Enlightenment of the 18th century, and the idea of a radical separation of Church and State is one enshrined in both the American Constitution and in the putative European one. After a century of absolutist totalitarianism, the dark shadow of 'enlightened' secularism, the attitudes of the Enlightenment are perhaps as passé as those which still make the United Kingdom the last *ancien régime* with a state religion (no longer reflecting the majority of the population) and a monarch who is head of that Church. When the heir to the throne talks about being a 'Defender of Faiths', many old animosities – and the deeply ingrained anti-Catholicism – of the English identity reappear.

The contemporary importance of religion is clearly embedded in the historical context and will not go away. A recent poll of the ten worst figures in English history included two medieval archbishops of Canterbury (Becket and Arundel) and a failed theological student (Titus Oates). The Tudors, especially as presented by the ubiquitous David Starkey, remain, as they have for a generation, the favoured historical dynasty for students and readers of all ages, and the Tudor Age, especially the much-studied reign of Henry VIII, is dominated by religious matters which beg many questions about today's England. The 2005 'celebrations', if that is the right word, of the failed Gunpowder Plot of 1605 have raised not only the question of the crucial role of anti-Catholicism in the English psyche, but the whole question of the association between terrorism and what is perceived as religious fundamentalism. Indeed, it has become a cliché to describe religion, dismissed as an irrelevance in other categories, as the source of all harm in the world.

In response to this milieu, Christians, and Catholic Christians in particular, tend to gather in a 'holy huddle' and fail to engage in what is not only perhaps a scramble for the survival of the Christian Church in the developed world, but also a conflict for the soul of society. 'Non-aggression' has become a Christian virtue (at least outside the lunatic fringes) and is often justified by the importance of 'humility' or the spiritual progress of the individual Christian in imitation of Christ. Humility should never be confused with timidity. Christians are called to witness the Gospel, proclaim its message and convert the world. If Christians have something to offer the world, they should make sure that their voice is heard. Proclamation and celebration of God's word and the teaching of the Church are especially important in a world where much is said and little understood about the basics of Christianity and its rich and nuanced tradition. The integrity, rationality and common sense of the true ancient wisdom of Christianity make a formidable whole, and, as the Cambridge historian Maurice Cowling has suggested in his exhaustive survey of Britain's religious thought, the three-volume *Religion and Public Doctrine in Modern England*, nothing has either superseded or demolished Christianity. What has been lacking, he suggests, is effective clarity and proclamation. Too often, Christian intellectuals have been seduced by transient and modish systems which lack the lasting appeal of the Gospel. Too often, also, they discover and make extensive use of a tired and rapidly dated modishness, mistaking 'relevance' for yesterday's ideas. There is a need today, as in all ages, for a coherent and fully articulated Christian philosophy, a Thomas Aquinas for our time. This may be found in some unexpected places.

Our age is a very visual one and the traditional Catholic 'beauty of holiness' is an important perception for the early 21st century. The humanism of the Renaissance, the explosion of the printed word since the Reformation, the 'rationalism' of the Enlightenment, were all primarily verbal phenomenon. Now film, sight and sound are equally compelling. The Church must present its aesthetic with the use of adequate technology, without the temptation, as in its encounter with modern thought, to go for the 'flashy' and the ephemeral; but it must also present the treasures of its artistic tradition, which remain unsurpassed. Christian art and architecture make a great impact in our visual culture. Simon Jenkins' *Thousand Best Churches*, however, reveals not only the power of the Christian heritage of this country, but also the danger of divorcing the 'meaning' of the Christian aesthetic from its artistic expression.

What is needed is a God-filled aesthetic, not a post-Christian one. Technology may be pointing the way. 'In some ways', Bristol sociologist Dr Kieran Flanagan has pointed out, 'digital culture has undermined the retina of the eye to look. New ways of seeing salvation have to be formulated, for the times are changing and the sites for sight are shifting. Unexpectedly, in the light of technology, the new twilight zones hover for the eye to glimpse in glimmers. These might incline in a theological direction. The issue of virtual reality has changed the way the seen and unseen are to be seen.'[1]

The extraordinary success of Dan Brown's novel, *The Da Vinci Code*, suggests how beguiling and bewitching puzzle-solving and conspiracy theories can be. *The Da Vinci Code* may be a tissue of historical half-truths, but its impact is based less on its historical authenticity than a strange contemporary desire to believe anything that is dressed up in the trappings of religion. It may be fiction but for many it is 'the real thing'. Symbolic thought, the exploration of mystery beyond words, has long been an essential part of the Christian endeavour. Poetry is often the language of theology and should be of liturgy (at least when banality has been excluded), and metaphor its handmaiden. In the Christian view of things symbol serves as a pointer to a richer and deeper reality, in contrast to the alternative thought-system of the world of *The Da Vinci Code* where symbol exists for its own sake. The sacramentality of Christ's presence in the world and in the life of the Church, implicit in the fundamental Christian doctrine of the Incarnation, unlocks a new, richer understanding of the worth of things. Recapturing this perspective is essential to appeal to the world of our time. Symbol and sacrament, in their truest sense, have to be rediscovered and redefined.

What is an appropriate model for the Church in a world where the technological revolution has not been accompanied by an increase of optimism? 'Inter-active' responses to this question will probably have stronger contemporary resonance than some still prevalent paradigms. The Communion of the Saints, for example, may make sense for a society which has a 'worldwide web'. On the other hand, in the light of global warming, the 20th-century's favourite model of the Church, as 'a pilgrim people', reflecting a world where 'progress' (perceived as personal, material and scientific) was highly esteemed, may not now be so compelling a view as a rediscovery of the medieval model of Noah's Ark. This expresses a delicate attempt to keep ecological balance in a storm-tossed and vulnerable world – made possible by collaboration with the creator God. A Christian environmentalism, with strong emphasis on stewardship and shared responsibility, has a strong attraction which has been glimpsed by all political parties as they vie for 'green' credibility.

The Latin *Cultura* can be translated in part as the cultivation of crops, and thus includes environmental matters. Culture in its widest meaning includes our total environment, our whole way of life. The relationship between Faith and Culture has become an increasingly important thread in Catholic thought. The writings of the Jesuit Michael Paul Gallagher are crucial here, and the subject has had a popular boost with the recent book of Professor Michael Burleigh, who has identified many post-Enlightenment movements and ideas as varieties of secular religion. In resisting the continuing onslaught of 'Fascist liberalism' and what could be the dying (but no less deadly) gasps of militant secularism, the Church needs to reassert its creative role in culture by 'recreating a living Christian Culture for our time'.[2]

In providing real supports for community, Christianity provides one of its strongest gifts to the modern world. Unfortunately, through overuse and stretching the word far beyond its linguistic boundaries, the danger of cliché is very strong in any discussion of 'community', but if based on Gospel values, and in particular on the common life of the early Christians (one of shared resources and mutual care), it can appeal to the sense of what being truly human is all about.

Much can be learnt here from those Christians who codified ways of life within the Christian tradition, legislators for 'holy living' like St Benedict and St Ignatius Loyola. St Benedict's self-regulating and more or less self-sufficient 'School of the Lords' Service' is a sixth-century response to the abiding problem of human isolation and the inadequate natural safeguards for the problems of living together. A Christian community, like Benedict's early monasteries, could be seen as a paradisal garden, or more appropriately, perhaps, as an oasis in a hostile and barren world. Benedict seems to achieve the impossible by making his monastery both exclusive and hospitable. For Hans Urs Von Baltasar, Christian 'islands of humanity' could help to 'humanise whatever is threatening to slide into the inhuman'.

If Christian symbol points beyond itself to God, so also Christian communities attempt to emulate the fuller community of the kingdom of God and seek union with the Creator in prayer. Christian prayer is at the centre of each Christian community, and the rediscovery of the force of prayer may be the instrument which finally completes the conversion of England so tentatively inaugurated by the gentle Roman monk Augustine at the end of the sixth century. Christian prayer, in all its variety – liturgical, personal, mental, contemplative – can be taught and rediscovered. If the Christian community could be a school of prayer so much could be achieved. Western culture has lost its spiritual dynamo and lost confidence in its own religious past. Too often men and women have found it easier to embrace a half-understood anaemic Eastern spirituality, cut off from its cultural roots and complications, than to explore their Christian heritage. We should look to our rich tradition: praying for the world, praying for the dead, encountering God in conversation – these can appeal to those whose life lacks nothing but a spiritual heart.

The mission of the Christian Church has always been to provide a heart for the world.

This essay reflects St Benedict's dictum that an abbot should present things old and new to his monks. The nation that forgets its God is one that neglects its true identity and tradition. A Benedictine monastery is a place for the few rather than the many, and despite St Bernard of Clairvaux's 12th-century hope that all men and women might enter the cloister, I feel sure that if that happened the world (for obvious reasons) would not have a very long future. What I am suggesting rather is something more like bringing the Christian message of hope, peace and meaning from the cloister to the world.

The sacredness of all things; the place of prayer in making sense of our everyday life; the deep reality of the sacraments in our lives: these are three overarching themes which emerge from my thoughts.

I hope they make sense in a world which is crying out for meaning.

CONTRIBUTORS BIOGRAPHIES

CHAPTER 1: EDWARD LEIGH

Edward Leigh worked in the private office of Mrs Thatcher from 1976–77 as private secretary in charge of her correspondence as Leader of the Opposition.

In the June 1983 General Election he was elected as Member of Parliament for Gainsborough & Horncastle. From 1983–85 he was Joint Secretary of the Conservative Parliamentary Defence Committee and the Parliamentary Agriculture Committee. Until early 1985 he was Chairman of the National Council for Civil Defence and Director of the Coalition For Peace Through Security. From 1990–93 he was a Parliamentary Under Secretary of State, Department of Trade and Industry. Prior to that he was a Parliamentary Private Secretary in the Home Office.

In May 1997 he was elected Member of Parliament for the new seat of Gainsborough with a majority of 6826. In 2005 this was increased to 8003. From 1995 to 2000 he was a member of the Social Security Select Committee, and from 1997 to 2001 Joint Vice-Chairman of the Conservative Party Parliamentary Foreign Affairs Committee.

Since July 2001 Edward has been Chairman of the Public Accounts Select Committee (PAC). In 2003 he founded the Cornerstone Group, a 'socially conservative' association of fellow Conservative MPs, which launched its own website in 2007.

In 1979 he published *Right Thinking*, an anthology of Tory quotations. In 2005 he published a pamphlet setting out his political philosophy: *The Strange Desertion of Tory*

England: The Conservative Alternative to the Liberal Orthodoxy, and later that year contributed to another pamphlet by parliamentary members of Cornerstone: *Being Conservative: A Cornerstone of Policies to Revive Tory Britain*. These pamphlets can be accessed on the website: http://cornerstonegroup.wordpress.com/press-releases/

CHAPTER 2: ALEXANDER BOOT

Alexander Boot is the author of *How the West Was Lost* (I.B. Tauris, 2006), on which this essay is based. A graduate of Moscow University, he had lectured on English and American literature, wrote criticism and got into trouble with the KGB before emigrating in 1973 – only to find that the West he was seeking was no longer there. This inspired a life-long quest for an explanation, reflected in numerous essays for British and US publications. He now divides his time between London and Burgundy, finishing a book on the folly of Tolstoy's faith and thought (*His Own God*).

CHAPTER 3: PETER MULLEN

The Rev. Dr Peter Mullen is Rector of St Michael, Cornhill, St Sepulchre-without-Newgate and Chaplain to the Stock Exchange, to six livery companies of the City of London and to the Royal Regiment of Fusiliers. He has served as a priest for 37 years in town and country and since 1998 in London. He is the author of some 40 books – fact and fiction – a frequent broadcaster and the contributor of numerous articles to the national and international press, as well as many pieces for theological and philosophical journals.

CHAPTER 4: BISHOP MICHAEL NAZIR-ALI

Bishop Michael Nazir-Ali is the 106th Bishop of Rochester. He holds both Pakistani and British citizenship. He has studied and taught at a number of leading universities in different parts of the world. He has worked as a priest and as a bishop in both the United Kingdom and Pakistan. After assisting the Archbishop of Canterbury for the 1988 Lambeth Conference, he became General Secretary of the Church Mission Society.

In 1994 he was appointed Bishop of Rochester. He entered the House of Lords in 1999.

He has a continuing interest in the role of religion in public life, mission and development issues, and also in inter-faith dialogue. Until recently he was a member of the Human Fertilisation and Embryology Authority and Chair of its Ethics and Law Committee. He has recently chaired the Church of England's Working Party on women in the episcopate and is President of the Anglican Communion's Network for Inter-Faith concerns (NIFCON). He has been a long-standing member of ARCIC (The Anglican-Roman Catholic Commission on Unity and Mission). He is Chair of the House of Bishops' Theological Group.

He has written several books on theology, Christian mission and culture and inter-faith issues. He was Chair of the Group that wrote *The Search for Faith* (Church House Publishing, 1996) and *Presence and Prophecy* (CHP, 2002). He has written several books and numerous articles. His books include *Citizens and Exiles* (SPCK, 1998), *Shapes of the Church to Come* (Kingsway, 2001), *Understanding My Muslim Neighbour* (Canterbury Press, 2002, with Chris Stone), and *Conviction and Conflict Islam, Christianity and World Order* (Continuum, 2006).

CHAPTER 5: ROGER SCRUTON

Roger Scruton is a writer, philosopher and public commentator. He engages in contemporary political and cultural debates from the standpoint of a conservative thinker and is well known as a powerful polemicist. He is currently Research Professor for the Institute for the Psychological Sciences, where he teaches philosophy at their Catholic graduate school in both Washington and Oxford.

Many of Roger Scruton's most recent books, such as *England: an Elegy, The West and the Rest, Gentle Regrets – Thoughts from a life and Culture Counts – Faith and Feeling in a World Besieged*, confront the cultural consequences of religion or the lack of it, in secular western culture: http://www.roger-scruton.com

CHAPTER 6: BAT YE'OR

Since 1971 Bat Ye'or has written numerous articles and books on the legal status of Jews and Christians in Islamized Christian lands. Her books have examined the demographic, sociological, political, economic and cultural factors leading, as she sees it, to the transformation of a Judaeo-Christian civilisation into an Islamic one. For this historical evolution she has coined the term 'dhimmitude'. Her main books in English are: *The Dhimmi: Jews and Christians under Islam* (1985); *The Decline of Eastern Christianity under Islam. From Jihad to Dhimmitude*; *Islam and Dhimmitude: Where Civilizations Collide* (2002) examines the European trend towards dhimmitude in the 20th century; *Eurabia: The Euro-Arab Axis* (2005) describes the modern manifestations of 'the perennial and fixed jihad-dhimmitude framework within Europe today'.

CHAPTER 7: CANON PETER WILLIAMS

Peter Williams is an Anglican clergyman. He taught Church History at Trinity College, Bristol for many years. He was founding editor of *Anvil*. His particular academic interest is in the history of Christian mission. He has written one book (*The Ideal of the Self-Governing Church: A Study in Victorian Missionary Strategy)* and contributed to many books and journals. He has also been a practitioner of mission as a vicar of a large, suburban parish in Sheffield. He is now a minister in Jersey. He is convinced of the central importance of listening to God's Word in its original cultural context and then seeking to explore its meaning, application and relevance to our contemporary culture. He is a Canon Emeritus of Sheffield Cathedral.

CHAPTER 8: SHUSHA GUPPY

Shusha Guppy was born into a traditional family in Teheran, Iran. In her teens she went to Paris to study at the Sorbonne. Following her marriage to English writer and explorer Nicholas Guppy in the 1960s, she moved to London where she has lived and worked ever since.

In the 1960s and 1970s she worked as a freelance writer, contributing to major publications on both sides of the Atlantic. Her first book, *The Blindfold Horse* (William Heinemann, 1988), won both the Yorkshire Post Prize for best non-fiction book, and a prize from the Royal Society of Literature. In France it was published under the title of *Un Jardin a Teheran* (Phebus), and won the Grand Prix Litteraire de Elle. It was followed by *A Girl in Paris* (William Heinemann, 1991), which was equally well-received, as was *Looking Back – A Panoramic View of a Literary Age* (Simon & Schuster). In 2000 she travelled in the Middle East, an experience which resulted in her travel book *Three Journeys in the Levant* (Starhaven). Her latest book was *The Secret of Laughter – Folk-tales and Fairy-tales from Classical Persia* (I.B. Tauris, 2005).

As a broadcaster Shusha Guppy made documentary films, of which *People of the Wind*, a documentary about the Bakhtiari tribes of Southern Iran, won an Oscar nomination for best documentary.

For 20 years until 2005 Shusha was London Editor of America's *The Paris Review*. Over the years she made and appeared in many radio and television programmes, and contributed frequently to BBC Radio. Shusha Guppy died in March 2008.

CHAPTER 9: PHILIPPA TAYLOR

Philippa Taylor is Senior Researcher on Bioethics, Marriage and the Family for CARE Trust. She is a member of the Family Law Review for the Centre for Social Justice and is currently studying for an MA in Bioethics. She has also been Associate Director at the Centre for Bioethics and Public Policy (CBPP). As well as doing some media work and presentations, she has written many of CARE's resources on the family, including numerous consultation responses, briefing papers, articles and booklets, including *For Better or For Worse: Marriage and Cohabitation Compared,* 2005, CARE (now in its 3rd edition), and *Counting the Cost: The Effects of Family Breakdown.*

CHAPTER 10: JOHN MARKS

Professor John Marks OBE has degrees in Science and the History and Philosophy of Science from Cambridge University, and a PhD in Nuclear Physics from London University. He has written extensively on education; has been a governor of a comprehensive school since 1978; and has over 40 years teaching experience in universities, polytechnics and schools. He has served on the Schools Examination and Assessment Council (1990–93), the National Curriculum Council (1992–93) and the Schools Curriculum & Assessment Authority (1993–97), and has been awarded the OBE for services to education. In 2007 he was appointed Professor of Education at the University of Buckingham.

CHAPTER 11: ARCHBISHOP VINCENT NICHOLS

The Most Reverend Vincent Nichols, Archbishop of Birmingham, was ordained to the Priesthood for the Archdiocese of Liverpool on 21 December 1969. He studied at the English College, Rome, the University of Manchester (MA) and Loyola University, Chicago (Med). Subsequently, he was a priest in St Anne's Parish in the Toxteth area of Liverpool and in 1980 appointed Director of Upholland Northern Institute, a provincial centre for Adult Education. He served for eight years as the General Secretary of the Bishops' Conference of England and Wales, and was ordained Bishop of North London in 1992. In 1998 he was appointed as Chairman of the Bishops' Conference Department for Catholic Education and Formation, and also Chairman of the Catholic Education Service. He was installed as Archbishop of Birmingham on 29 March 2000.

CHAPTER 12: ABBOT AIDAN BELLENGER

Dom Aidan Bellenger has been a monk of the Benedictine abbey of Downside in Somerset since 1982 and Abbot since 2006. He has worked in Downside School as a teacher of History, a housemaster and headmaster. He was Prior of Downside for five years and has been a parish priest for more than a decade. He has a doctorate from Cambridge in

Ecclesiastical History and is a Fellow of the Royal Historical Society and the Society of Antiquaries, as well as President of the English Catholic Historical Association. Widely published, he thinks that Catholic Faith and sound historical scholarship are complementary, and that the secularism of culture is undermining our understanding of the past.

NOTES

CHAPTER 1

1. Quoted by Victoria Combe, *Daily Telegraph*, 6 September 2001.

2. Bishop of Manchester, Rt Rev. Nigel McCulloch, quoted by Ruth Gledhill, *The Times*, 20 March 2004.

3. Quoted by Victoria Combe, *Daily Telegraph*, 6 September 2001.

4. Cited by Jonathan Petre, 'Muslims will soon outnumber Anglicans', *Daily Telegraph*, 28 October 2001.

5. Ibid.

6. Pope Benedict XVI (as Cardinal Ratzinger), interview, *La Repubblica*, 19 November 2004.

7. Matthew d'Ancona, *Sunday Daily Telegraph*, 'The Davids await their fate in a frenzied market', 16 October 2005.

8. Aleister Crowley, *Book of the Law* (1909), l. 40.

9. Gen. 3:5.

10. Robert Whelan, *The Necessary Family and How to Support it*, p.24, 1996.

11. Extrapolation from ONS online figures for 2004.

12. *Home Office (2006) Violent Crime Overview, Homicide and Gun Crime 2004/2005: Supplementary Volume to Crime in England and Wales 2004/2005.*

13. Office of National Statistics. The actual figure was an increase from 6.9 per 100,000 population in 1991 to 13 in 2004. The number of alcohol-related deaths has more than doubled in the same period, from 4144 to 8380.

14. Office of National Statistics figures, ONS online.

15. *Review 2001/2002: Building on Success, Youth Justice Board, London*: The Stationery Office (July 2002).

16. T. S. Eliot, Choruses from 'The Rock', 1934, in *The Complete Poems and Plays of T.S. Eliot*, 1969.

17. John 14:15.

18. Leen, *Why the Cross?*, p.9, 1941.

19. John 18:36.

20. 'In the end there is a judgement that, I think, if you have faith about these things, you realise that judgement is made by other people...and if you believe in God, it's made by God as well.' 'Blair "prayed to God" over Iraq', BBC News online, 3 March 2006.

21. Interview with Adam Boulton, 'Sunday Live', *Sky News*, 5 March 2006.

22. BBC News online, 'PM attacked on Iraq "God" remarks', 4 March 2006.

23. 'And on the seventh day Tony Blair created...', *Observer*, 3 August 2003.

24. Interview in *Vanity Fair*, May 2003.

25. Paxman interview with Blair, reported on BBC News online, 6 February 2003.

26. Interview with David Remnick, 'The real Mr Blair' (part two), *Observer,* 1 May 2005.

27. John Henry Newman, *Certain Difficulties felt by Anglicans in Catholic Teaching*, 1850, II. 197.

28. Edward Norman, *Anglican Difficulties: a New Syllabus of Errors*, 2004.

29. Bishop Hollis, interviewed on 'Newsnight', 20 April 2005.

30. Hannah Baker, 'Missionaries return to West Yorkshire', *Catholic Herald*, 14 July 2006.

31. Robyn Dixon, 'African Catholics seek a voice to match their growing strength', *Los Angeles Times*, 16 April 2006.

32. John 10:10.

33. John 8:31–32.

34. Luke 19:40.

CHAPTER 4

1. Hans Küng, *Global Responsibility In Search of a New World Ethic*, London, SCM, 1991, and in *Christianity and the World Religions*, London SCM, 1993, especially pp.xiif and pp.441f.

2. Samuel Huntington, *The Clash of Civilisations and the Remaking of World Order*, New York, Simon & Schuster, 1996, p.320.

3. See further Oliver O'Donovan, *Resurrection and Moral Order,* Leicester, IVP, 1986, pp.31ff.

4. James Ward, *The Realm of Ends: Pluralism and Theism*, CUP, 1912, esp. pp.97ff.

5. See further *Life in Christ: Morals, Communion and the Church*, Anglican-Roman Catholic International Commission, CHP, CTS, 1994, pp.3ff. See also *The Family Way* in the *Cambridge Alumni Magazine* (CAM) Lent, 2000, No. 29, pp.19f.

6. On this issue, see Michael Banner, *Christian Ethics and Contemporary Moral Problems*, CUP, 1999, pp.270ff.

7. Richard Hooker, *The Laws of Ecclesiastical Polity* (ed. Arthur Pollard), Manchester, Fyfield, 1990, Book I, pp.34ff.

8. Gerhard von Rad, *Genesis*, London, SCM, 1972, pp.59ff.

9. Lahore, Ashraf, 1969, p.132.

10. W. R. Sorley and G. F. Stout (eds), *Essays in Philosophy*, CUP, 1927, pp.204ff.

11. See further *Personal Origins*, The Report of a Working Party on Human Fertilisation and Embryology, BSR, London, CHP, 2nd edition, 1996, pp.32ff.

12. Pete Moore, *Babel's Shadow: Genetic Technologies in a Fracturing Society*, Oxford, Lion, 1999, pp.154ff. On the 'developmental' view of personhood, see John Habgood, *Being a Person: Where Faith and Science Meet*, London, Hodder, 1998.

13. In *Christian Ethics and Contemporary Moral Problems*, op cit., pp.68ff.

14. Based on results presented at the *Symposium on Organ Donation and Transplantation The Multi-Faith Perspective*, Bradford, March 2000.

15. In *Religion Within the Limits of Reason Alone*, Harper, New York, 1960, pp.6, 131, 170ff.

16. See particularly Articles 8, 10 and 11.

CHAPTER 6

1. Henry Laurent, 'Le Mufti et la France de la IVe République', *Revue d'Etudes Palestiniennes,* 81, Paris (Autumn 2001), pp.70–87; David Pryce-Jones, *Betrayal: France, the Arabs, and the Jews,* New York, Encounter Books: 2006, pp.60–67.

2. Bat Ye'or, *Eurabia, The Euro-Arab Axis,* Madison, NJ: Fairleigh Dickinson University Press, 2005, p.52.

3. MEDEA, European Institute for Research on Mediterranean and Euro-Arab Cooperation with the support of the European Commission.

4. *The Dialogue,* p.23, parentheses in the text. Report of the High-level Group, 13 November 2006. Members of the High-level Advisory Group: Joint chair, Assia Alaouibensalah, Jean Daniel. Members: Malek Chebel, Juan Diez Nicolas, Umberto Eco, Shmuel N. Eisenstadt, George Joffe, Ahmed Kamal Aboulmagd, Bichara Khader, Adnan Wafic Kassar, Pedrag Matvejevic, Rostane Mehdi, Fatima Mernissi, Tariq Ramadan, Faruk Sen, Faouzi Skali, Simone Susskind-Weinberger, Tullia Zevi. Working group assisting the High-level Advisory Group: Léonce Bekemans, Yudhishthir Raj Isar, Philippe Ratte.

5. Anna Lindh, Swedish Social Democrat Foreign Minister (1998–2003), whose 'hatred of Israel can only be described as almost pathological', according to Zvi Mazel, the then Israeli Ambassador to Sweden; see Manfred Gerstenfeld, *European-Israeli Relations: Between Confusion and Change?,* Jerusalem Centre for Public Affairs, Jerusalem, 2006. She was killed by Mijailo Mijailovic, a mentally disturbed Serbian. Lindh was greatly admired and praised by her European colleagues and by the Palestinians.

6. 'Peace be upon him', a benediction formula used by pious Muslims.

7. Gerald M. Steinberg, www.ngo-monitor.org

8. European Commission: 'A Soul for Europe'.

9. Statement of Dr Traugott Schoefthaler, Barcelona VIII Conference of Ministers of Foreign Affairs, Tampere, 28 November 2006.

10. www.unaoc.org

11. http://www.spiegel.de/international/germany/0,1518,474629,00.html, 29 March 2007.

12. Tony Blair, 'A Battle for Global Values', *Foreign Affairs*, London, January 2007.
13. According to a report in the *International Herald Tribune*, 8 January 2007.

CHAPTER 7

1. Roger Anstey, 1975, *The Atlantic Slave Trade and British Abolition, 1760–1810*, Macmillan, p.41.
2. Niall Ferguson, *Empire: How Britain Made the Modern World*, 2003, Allen Lane, p.83.
3. Ferguson, 2003, p.117.
4. Anstey, 1975, p.406.
5. Anstey, 1975, p.104.
6. Anstey, 1975, p.117.
7. David W. Bebbington, 1989, *Evangelicalism in Modern Britain: A History from the 1730s to the 1980s*, Routledge, p.60.
8. Bebbington, 1989, p.71.
9. Anstey, 1975, p.191.
10. John Newton, for example, was an evangelical Christian for many years before he became convinced of the case for the abolition of slavery (see Ferguson, 2003, p.74).
11. John Wesley, 1774, *Thoughts Upon Slavery* (pamphlet), R. Hawes, Vol. 6.
12. D. B. Davis, 1984, *Slavery and Human Progress*, Oxford University Press.
13. Anstey, 1975, p.198.
14. Anstey, 1975, p.199.
15. Anstey, 1975, 175, note 45.
16. My italics, Anstey, 1975, p.197.
17. Tomkins, 2007, *William Wilberforce: a biography*, Lion Hudson, pp.11–12.
18. Anstey, 1975, p.218.
19. Wesley, 1774, Vol. 3.
20. Richard S. Reddie, 2007 (*Abolition: The Struggle to Abolish Slavery in the British Colonies*, Lion, pp.137–38), thinks so, but Steve Turner (2002, *Amazing Grace: the Story of America's Most Beloved Song*, Ecco Books, New York) dates his commitment to abolition in the mid-eighties (p.126).
21. Anstey, 1975, p.233.
22. E. M. Howse, 1953, *Saints in Politics: 'The Clapham Sect' and the Growth of Freedom*, Open University, p.11.
23. Reddie, 2007, p.140.
24. Anstey, 1975, p.255.
25. Wesley, 1774, Vol. 1.
26. Kevin Belmonte, 2002, *Hero for Humanity: A Biography of William Wilberforce*, Navpress, p.58.
27. Anstey, 1975, p.174.
28. Belmonte, 2002, p.91.
29. Belmonte, 2002, p.94.

30. Belmonte, 2002, p.84.
31. Belmonte, 2002, p.90.
32. Belmonte, 2002, p.86.
33. Belmonte, 2002, p.87.
34. Howse, 1953, p.32.
35. Anstey, 1975, p.251.
36. Anstey, 1975, p.301.
37. Anstey, 1975, p.406.
38. Anstey, 1975, p.408.
39. Anstey, 1975, p.275.
40. Belmonte, 2002, p.100.
41. Belmonte, 2002, p.273.
42. John Coffey, 2006, *The Abolition of the Slave Trade: Christian Conscience and Political Action,* Cambridge Papers, Vol. 15, No. 2, June 2006.
43. Hochschild, 2006, *Bury the Chains: the British Struggle to Abolish Slavery*, Pan Books, p.366.
44. Coffey, 2006.
45. Belmonte, 2002, p.112.
46. Howse, 1953, p.165.

CHAPTER 8

1. Reported to the author by Martin Lings (1909–2005), British Sufi Muslim convert, author of many books on Sufism and related matters, including a highly acclaimed life of Mohammed (*Muhammad*, Harper Collins, 1983), and *Shakespeare in the Light of Sacred Art* (Allen and Unwin, 1966).
2. Reported to the author by Martin Lings.
3. http://news.bbc.co.uk/2/hi/uk_news/6359363.stm, 'UK is accused of failing children', 14 February 2007, BBC News Online.

CHAPTER 9

1. Hebrews 13:4. All Bible references are taken from the New International Version.
2. Jade Jagger, *Daily Mail*, 25 June 1997.
3. 'Geldof: two parents are best', *The Times*, October 2004.
4. D. Popenoe, *The State of Our Unions*, Rutgers, 2005.
5. D. Marsland, *Reclaiming the Family*, ed. R. Segalman, Paragon, 1998.
6. S. Callan, *A Brief History of Marriage*, www.2-in-2–1.co.uk/articles
7. Ibid.
8. Such as 'jumping the broom' and 'living tally'.
9. S. Coontz, 'The World Historical Transformation of Marriage', *Journal of Marriage and Family* 66, 2004.
10. Hugh of St Victor, 12th century, quoted in C. Ash, *Marriage: Sex in the Service of God*, IVP, 2003.
11. C. Ash, *Marriage: Sex in the Service of God*, IVP, 2003.
12. D. Browning & E. Marquardt, *Liberal Cautions on Same-Sex Marriage*, 2004, paper presented to Witherspoon Institute.

13. These were partly as a result of trends such as the decline in agricultural labour, mortality rates and the movement of married women into the paid workforce, along with events such as the Depression and the Second World War.

14. A. Cherlin, The Deinstitutionalisation of American Marriage, *Journal of Marriage and Family* 66, November 2004.

15. Ibid.

16. Ibid.

17. Schluter & Lee, *The R Factor*, 1993, quoted in C. Ash, *Marriage: Sex in the Service of God*, IVP, 2003.

18. C. Ash, *Marriage: Sex in the Service of God*, IVP, 2003.

19. Kathryn Edin & Maria Kefalas, 2005, *Promises I Can Keep: Why Poor Women Put Motherhood Before Marriage*, University of California Press.

20. A. Cherlin, The Deinstitutionalisation of American Marriage, *Journal of Marriage and Family* 66, November 2004.

21. D. Browning & E. Marquardt, *Liberal Cautions on Same-Sex Marriage*, 2004, paper presented to Witherspoon Institute.

22. C. Smart & P. Stevens, *Cohabitation Breakdown*, London: Family Policy Studies Centre, 2000.

23. M. Johnson, 'Commitment in Personal Relationships' in W. Jones & D. Perlman (eds), *Advances in Personal Relationships: A Research Annual*, Jessica Kingsley Publishers, London, Vol. 3, 1991.

24. J. Ermisch, *Trying Again: Repartnering after Dissolution of a Union*, Working Paper of the Institute for Social and Economic Research, Paper 2002–19.

25. House of Commons Written Answer, Hansard, 8 May 2000: Column: 262W.

26. S. Stanley, *Sliding Versus Deciding: Inertia and the Premarital Cohabitation Effect*, Family Relations, 55, October 2006.

27. C. Ash, *Marriage: Sex in the Service of God*, IVP, 2003.

28. Not necessarily monogamous marriage.

29. D. Browning & E. Marquardt, *Liberal Cautions on Same-Sex Marriage*, 2004, paper presented to Witherspoon Institute.

30. Matthew 19:4–6 quoting from Genesis 1:27, 2:24.

31. The Notice of Marriage by Certificate, signed by couples getting married in a Register Office: 'Marriage according to the law of this country is the union of one man with one woman, voluntarily entered into for life, to the exclusion of all others.'

32. 'To cleave' is not used here to mean 'to split', which is a common English language usage of the word, but instead, as explained in the text, here it means 'to cling' or 'stick to'.

33. Genesis 1–11, D. Atkinson, *Bible Speaks Today* series, IVP, 1990.

34. E.g., Malachi 2:14 '...*The Lord is acting as the witness between you and the wife of your youth ... she is your partner, the wife of your marriage covenant.*'

35. O'Donovan, 1994, quoted in C. Ash, *Marriage: Sex in the Service of God*, IVP, 2003.

36. Ibid.

37. C. Ash, *Marriage: Sex in the Service of God*, IVP, 2003.

38. A. Oswald, *The Extraordinary Effects of Marriage*, Warwick University, January 2002.

39. L. Waite & M. Gallagher, *The Case For Marriage: Why Married People are Happier, Healthier and Better Off Financially*, Doubleday, 2000.

40. A. Oswald & D. Blanchflower, Well Being over Time in Britain and the US, 2002, *Journal of Public Economics*, Vol. 88, July 2004.

41. C. Wilson & A. Oswald, *How Does Marriage Affect Physical and Psychological Health? A Survey of the Longitudinal Evidence*, Warwick Economic Research Papers, revised version, 2005.

42. C. Wilson & A. Oswald, *How Does Marriage Affect Physical and Psychological Health? A Survey of the Longitudinal Evidence*, January 2002.

43. Families of England and Wales, Census 2001, ONS.

44. *Marriage in 21st century Britain and Europe*, Centre for Research in Social Policy, August 2004.

45. Jill Kirby, *The Price of Parenthood*, Centre for Policy Studies, 2005.

46. *Freedom's Orphans: Raising Youth in a Changing World*, IPPR Report.

47. S. Callan, *Sociological Perspectives on the Family*, 2006.

48. *Population Trends* 117, Autumn 2004, Office of National Statistics.

49. The Millennium Cohort Study interviewed 15,000 mothers. H. Benson, *The conflation of marriage and cohabitation in government statistics – a denial of difference rendered untenable by an analysis of outcomes*, 2006.

50. *Population Trends* 117, Autumn 2004, Office of National Statistics.

51. H. Benson (2006). Age is another risk factor for relationship breakdown; however, marital status still has such a strong influence that even younger married mothers are more stable than older cohabiting mothers.

52. S. Callan, *Sociological Perspectives on the Family*, 2006.

53. S. Marquardt, *Between Two Worlds: The Inner Lives of Children of Divorce,* 2005.

54. Callan, *Fractured Families,* Report on Family Breakdown for the Centre for Social Justice, 2006.

55. P. Amato, The consequences of divorce for adults and children. *Journal of Marriage and Family*, 62, 2000.

56. Berthoud & Gershuny, eds, *Seven Years in the Lives of British Families*, Policy Press, 2000.

57. Ibid.

58. Anastasia de Waal, 'Wedding Day Rebellion', *Guardian*, 16 February 2006.

59. Ibid.

60. Report from a *Joint ESRC/ONS/BSPS seminar on the implications of demographic change*, Population Trends 125, Autumn 2006.

61. Kathryn Edin & Maria Kefalas, *Promises I Can Keep: Why Poor Women Put Motherhood Before Marriage,* 2005. The authors observed that women are fearful of failing in a marriage and prefer to wait until they are more secure economically. Smock (2004), however, notes that financial barriers to marriage are not just felt among the low-income population.

62. Shaun Bailey, 'The reason our streets are so violent', *Daily Telegraph*, 19 January 2006.

63. Carlson, Family structure, father involvement, and adolescent behaviour outcomes, *Journal of Marriage and Family*, 68, 2006.

64. R. O'Neill, *Experiments in Living: The Fatherless Family*, Civitas, 2002.

65. S. McLanahan, *Fragile Families and Child Wellbeing: a birth cohort study* www.fragilefamilies.princeton.edu

66. Benson, 2006.

67. Ibid.

68. Promoting 'healthy' marriages acknowledges that some marriages are 'unhealthy' and teaches society (and parents) to distinguish between relationships that are good for people and those that are bad or 'unhealthy'. At the very least such programmes suggest that not all marriages are good for adults and children.

69. For example, much public comment focuses on divorce and not on the (more prevalent) breakdown of cohabitation. This itself contributes to the decline in the perception and standing of marriage.

70. Callan, *Fractured Families*, 2006.

71. M. Durham, *The Conservative Party, New Labour and the Politics of the Family*, Parliamentary Affairs 54, 2001.

72. Ibid.

73. E. Butler-Sloss, *Family Law Reform – opportunities taken, wasted and yet to be seized*, Bar Council Lecture, December 2005.

74. A third of unmarried couples would benefit, another third would benefit but would need extra help with drug/job problems etc, and a final third should not be encouraged to strengthen their relationship because of more severe problems, such as abuse, prison sentences etc.

75. *Equipping Britain for Our long-term Future: Financial Statement and Budget Report*, HM Treasury, July 1997.

76. For papers by D. Draper & L. Beighton, specific figures and press releases, see www.care.org.uk.

77. The ONS published a paper in March 2006 which found that there are 1.2 million couples 'living-apart together' and that 25 per cent of lone parents had a non-live-in partner. The Millennium Cohort Study found that out of 4629 unmarried families almost 1000 described themselves not as cohabiting but as 'closely involved', and a further 300 as 'just friends'.

78. *The Need to Restructure Tax Credits*, Draper & Beighton, CARE Policy Paper, www.care.org.uk

79. Findings from a presentation of a Care for the Family Young Adult project survey of young adults.

80. C. Ash, op. cit.

CHAPTER 10

1. *Daily Telegraph*, 27 September 2002; the study is *Reorganising Primary Classroom Learning* by Nigel Hastings & Karen Chantrey Wood, Open University Press.

2. J. Chall, *The Academic Achievement Challenge: What really works in the classroom,* Guilford Press, 2000, gives an authoritative account of the parallel controversy in the United States. See also J. E. Stone, 'Developmentalism: An Obscure but Pervasive Restriction on Educational Improvement', *Education Policy Analysis Archives*, Vol. 4, No. 8, April 1996, which analyses 'developmentalism' – one of the main causes of the retreat from teaching identified so persuasively by Melanie Phillips in schools in this country.

3. Melanie Phillips, 1996, Little, Brown.

4. J. Honey, *The Language Trap: race, class and the 'standard English' issue in British schools,* National Council for Educational Standards, 1983; J. Honey, *Language is Power: The Story of Standard English and its Enemies*, Penguin, 1998.

5. See the letter signed by 500 professors and lecturers in English in the THES when the National Curriculum for English was being revised in 1993.

6. Regular practice in mental arithmetic – once a daily feature of the primary school timetable – had largely disappeared until Sir Ron Dearing, then Chairman of the Schools Curriculum and Assessment Authority, forced through externally set mental arithmetic tests when the National Curriculum was being revised in 1993.

7. Some non-calculator papers, or sometimes non-calculator questions, are now part of National Curriculum tests and GCSE examinations, but there are not yet enough tests of this kind. Similarly some progress has been made in reducing the size of formulae lists, but more still needs to be done.

8. Further information on standards in arithmetic is given in Chapters 1 & 2 of J. Marks, *Standards of Arithmetic: How to correct the decline*, Centre for Policy Studies, 1996.

9. The Teaching of Number in three Inner-urban LEAs, *Ofsted, September 1997;* there has been virtually no improvement in the ten years since then (see P. Tymms, R. Coe and C. Merrell (University of Durham), *Standards in English schools: changes since 1997 and the impact of government policies and initiatives*, *Sunday Times*, April 2005).

10. *The Teaching of Reading in 45 Inner London Primary Schools – A report by Her Majesty's Inspectors in collaboration with the LEAs of Islington, Southwark and Tower Hamlets,* Ofsted, 1996; the study used standardised tests of reading for seven- and 11-year-olds in 45 primary schools.

11. J. Clare, 'A lesson in failure', *Daily Telegraph*, 2 December 2005; for further discussion of the Clackmannanshire study and a similar project in West Dunbartonshire, see T. Burkard, *The End of Illiteracy? The Holy Grail of Clackmannanshire*, Centre for Policy Studies, 2004, and T. Burkard, *A World First for West Dunbartonshire*, Centre for Policy Studies, 2006.

12. See the article by Minette Marrin, *The teachers' plot to make our children into failures*, from the *Daily Telegraph*, 17 December 1998, reprinted as an appendix to this essay.

13. J. Marks, *Standards of Arithmetic: How to correct the decline*, Centre for Policy Studies, 1996.

14. For further detail, see S. J. Prais, 'Improving School Mathematics in Practice', in *Mathematics Education,* The Gatsby Foundation, November 1995, especially pp.8–9.

15. G. Last, 'The Gatsby Primary Mathematics Project: A demonstration project in the London Borough of Barking and Dagenham', in *Mathematics Education,* The Gatsby Foundation, November 1995.

16. These textbooks are currently being marketed extensively in California – especially in the region of Silicon Valley, where many computer experts have despaired of the standards of mathematics teaching in Californian schools.

17. For further information, see J. Marks, *Science and the Making of the Modern World,* Heinemann Educational, 1983, Chapters 3.3 & 3.4.

18. T. Gardiner, *Observed effects of recent changes in English school mathematics on those entering universities at age 18,* University of Birmingham, 1994.

19. For a broader discussion relating to Mathematics in secondary and vocational as well as primary education, see S. J. Prais, *Productivity, Education & Training: An International Perspective,* Cambridge University Press, 1995, pp.75–90.

CHAPTER 12

1. K. Flanagan, *Visual Culture*, Basingstoke, 2004, p.89.

2. M. P. Gallagher, *Clashing Symbols*, 2nd edition, London, 2003, p.168.